Quotations in

Physics,
Philosophy and
Psychology

Compiled and
illustrated by

Claus Grupen

Cover illustration by Petra Peres, Vienna, based on an idea
of Cornelius Grupen and a draft of Claus Grupen;
with a preface from Sir Arnold Wolfendale, 14th Astronomer Royal, FRS;
and an introduction from Cornelius Grupen;
all portraits (created over a period of 50 years) from Claus Grupen;
copyrights with Claus Grupen;
Siegen, September 2010.

Quotations in Physics, Philosophy and Psychology

Compiled and illustrated
by Claus Grupen

Shaker Verlag
Aachen 2010

Bibliographic information published by the Deutsche Nationalbibliothek
The Deutsche Nationalbibliothek lists this publication in the Deutsche
Nationalbibliografie; detailed bibliographic data are available in the Internet
at http://dnb.d-nb.de.

ISBN 978-3-8322-9462-5
ISSN 0945-0947

Shaker Verlag GmbH • P.O. BOX 101818 • D-52018 Aachen
Phone: 0049/2407/9596-0 • Telefax: 0049/2407/9596-9
Internet: www.shaker.de • e-mail: info@shaker.de

Preface

Claus Grupen has put together an impressive collection of quotations from a variety of areas of human life – and covering two millennia. What a feast of wisdom and humour, not to mention the skilful sketches of some of the originators.

Inevitably the choice is conditioned by the author's own area of expertise and here we have those of a distinguished practitioner of high energy physics, both in the field of cosmic rays and in experiments with the giant accelerators. This is the reason for our hero, Albert Einstein, looming large in the book; he towered above the field of science, too.

It is a pleasure to commend this book. Not only can one be enlightened and amused by dipping in at random but by using the excellent index to choose a quote for any need. A relevant Quotation to close this brief Preface might be

'Only a wise man can distil the manifold utterances of others'

Here we have such a distillation.

Sir Arnold Wolfendale FRS
14th Astronomer Royal.

Acknowledgements

The quotations in this volume have been collected over the course of more than 40 years. I have used many of them in university lectures and popular science talks as well as in papers, articles, and books. In all cases, the objective was twofold: to amuse students and readers, and to put scientific findings into the wider perspective developed by the great thinkers in the history of ideas, from the earliest days of scientific enquiry in ancient Egypt and Greece to the present day. This is the first time I have gathered these quotes and sayings between two covers, but the twin objective remains unchanged: entertainment and enlightenment. To the extent that this has been achieved, it is my students' and readers' merit as much as my own. I thank them for encouraging me to keep spicing up my works with intelligent and humourous quotes.

My son, Dr. Cornelius Grupen, a historian of philosophy by training, was rather helpful in ordering the quotations and giving the whole collection of quotes a reasonable structure. One of my colleagues, Dr. Tilo Stroh, took over the Herculean job to arrange the quotations in a suitable way, to scrutinise the text, and to proofread everything. He also devoted much of his time to adjusting the scale and shape of the illustrations, to create an author and subject index, and, last not least, he polished the overall layout and gave the typesetting an attractive finish.

I am indebted to Rufus Neal from Cambridge University Press for proposing an interesting alternative alliteration for the book title. I thank Sönke Adlung from Oxford University Press for providing quotations from distinguished scientists. Finally I would like to thank Mark Rodgers from Durham University for checking the English of the introduction and the like.

Claus Grupen
Siegen/Germany, September 2010

Contents

Chapter 1

Introduction

I have a wretched memory, and when
any one makes a long speech to me I never
remember what he is talking about.
Having such a bad memory, I will ask
you to cut your answers shorter, if you
would take me with you.

Plato, Protagoras

Paradoxically, a few words often say more than many, and composing a pointed aphorism can take longer than writing a lengthy essay. The great 17th century polymath Blaise Pascal recognised the cost of curtness when he wrote: "I have only made this letter rather long because I have not had time to make it shorter." Similarly, St. Augustine apologised: "I might have made my reply in fewer words, but desiring to answer you at once, I think it better to write a long letter than incur loss of time." The church father knew that brevity is hard work, but also a sure sign of discipline and courtesy. While the common blabbermouth reveals his own confusion and wastes everyone's time, he who keeps his statements short shows respect for his audience by recognising their time is scarce and precious. As one would expect, Zeno the Cynic liked his statements short and simple, calling everyone who spoke at length or used ornate phrases a chatterbox. Plato, the secular patron saint of all wisdom and enquiry, was perhaps the greatest friend of brevity. He derided Protagoras, the superstar sophist, for his long speeches and admired the Spartans for their legendary concision. The Spartans' penchant for speaking to the point survives in our adjective "laconic", derived from the Greek lakonikos, a reference to the Spartan dominion in Southern Greece. When Philip of Macedonia came to raid the Laconian plain, he reportedly threatened: "If I win

1

this war, you will be slaves forever." The Spartan commander sent a one-word reply: "If."

While long texts and speeches may give us information, there is nothing like a short statement to capture insight. They say an image is worth a thousand words, but if the likes of Pascal and Plato are on to something, the same holds true for a single sentence: a handful of words may not only be worth as much as, but more than a thousand words. I know it sounds fishy from the point of view of old-school arithmetic, but the evidence is in what follows. Taking inspiration from Plato's very own tripartite model of the soul comprising desire, impulse and intellect, my father has gathered words of wisdom from the corresponding disciplines of psychology, physics and philosophy. I found them so rich in thought and honed in form that I couldn't help admit that less, indeed, can be more. Each quotation captures the essence of many pages of text, making this collection tantamount to an entire bookshelf.

To sound a note of caution, don't take offence at any misattribution or inaccuracy you may encounter. Precise citations and scholarly references are an invention of the very recent past. For millennia, Western thought has prospered without the aid of bibliography or footnote. In fact, the finest minds are often the sloppiest scribes. Let us follow the example set by the celebrated 17th century theologian and neo-Platonist philosopher Henry More. Most of the time, he couldn't be bothered to look up half-remembered passages of text and would revert to generous formulae such as "Somewhere in Aristotle, it says . . . " or "In one of the earlier dialogues, Socrates suggests . . . ". Why not take inspiration from Henry More's generosity? By enjoying a famous quotation without worrying too much about its source or provenance, we recognise that the truth lies not in the letter, but in the spirit. The spirit, not the letter? I wonder where I read that. I can't seem to remember. It must have been somewhere in St. Paul.

Cornelius Grupen
Hamburg, September 2010

1.1 Introductory Quotes

My sources are unreliable, but their information is fascinating.

Ashleigh Brilliant

Famous remarks are very seldom quoted correctly. Simeon Strunsky

Fancy wordings do not necessarily represent fancy insights.

Ludwig Marcuse

It is a good thing for an uneducated man to read books of quotations.

Sir Winston Churchill

Misquotation is, in fact, the pride and privilege of the learned. A widely-read man never quotes accurately, for the rather obvious reason that he has read too widely. Hesketh Pearson

A book of quotations can never be complete. Robert M. Hamilton

You are wise, witty and wonderful, but you spend too much time reading this sort of stuff. Frank Crane

Physics, Philosophy and Psychology – three fields ordered in increasing madness. Claus Grupen

Philosophy, Physics and Psychology could perhaps be made more widely accessible as Mind, Matter and Madness. Rufus Neal

Chapter 2

Physics Quotes

2.1 The Universe

I do believe in science as a human endeavour to increasingly unravel more and more about nature and life.
Johan Gielis

No human being is constituted to know the truth, the whole truth, and nothing but the truth; and even the best of men must be content with fragments, with partial glimpses, never the full fruition.
Sir William Osler

I have looked further into space than any human being did before me.
Sir Friedrich Wilhelm (William) Herschel

Sir Friedrich Wilhelm (William) Herschel

Equipped with his five senses, man explores the universe around him and calls the adventure science.
Edwin Powell Hubble

The universe is like a safe to which there is a combination. But the combination is locked up in the safe.
Peter de Vries

The greatest discoveries of science have always been those that forced us to re-think our beliefs about the Universe and our place in it.   Robert L. Park

Science is not merely a collection of facts, but is instead an ongoing detective story, in which scientists passionately search for clues in the hope of unraveling the mysteries of the universe.   Alan Guth

Cosmologists are claiming that they can extrapolate backward in time to learn the conditions in the universe just one second after the beginning! If cosmologists are so smart, you might ask, why can't they predict the weather? The answer, I would argue, is not that cosmologists are so smart, but that the early universe is much simpler than the weather!   Alan Guth

Either we've seen the birth of the universe, or we've seen a pile of pigeon shit. [On the discovery of the cosmological blackbody radiation with a large radio antenna and the associated noise problems]   Arno Penzias

One man's noise is another man's signal.   Sir Arnold Wolfendale

Now it is quite clear to me that there are no solid spheres in the heavens, and those that have been devised by the authors to save the appearances, exist only in the imagination.   Tycho Brahe

Tycho Brahe

Without continuous creation the universe must evolve toward a dead state in which all the matter is condensed into a vast number of dead stars.   Fred Hoyle

The present universe is something like the old professor nearing retirement with his brilliant future behind him.   Alan Sandage

Nature composes some of her loveliest poems for the microscope and the telescope.
Theodore Roszak

Telescopes are in some ways like time machines. They reveal galaxies so far away that their light has taken billions of years to reach us. We in astronomy have an advantage in studying the universe, in that we can actually see the past.
Sir Martin Rees

The phenomena of nature, especially those that fall under the inspection of the astronomer, are to be viewed, not only with the usual attention to facts as they occur, but with the eye of reason and experience.
Sir Friedrich Wilhelm (William) Herschel

The Doppler effect is responsible for the red shifts of distant galaxies, and also of quasars, and thus provides the best evidence for the expansion of the universe, as described by Hubble's law.
Columbia Encyclopedia

The energy you use to turn a single page of a book is more than all the radio telescopes have collected since the beginning of radio astronomy.
Jocelyn Burnell Judson

A friend of mine once showed a photograph of the Andromeda galaxy to the art director of a magazine on which he was working. The art director said, 'That's gorgeous! But can we get a shot of it from another angle?'
Anonymous

Great scientific discoveries have been made by men seeking to verify quite erroneous theories about the nature of things.
Aldous Huxley

Aldous Huxley

The physicist in preparing for his work needs three things, mathematics, mathematics, and mathematics.
Wilhelm Conrad Röntgen

Physicists are, as a general rule, highbrows. They think and talk in long, Latin words, and when they write anything down they usually include at least one partial differential and three Greek letters.   Stephen White

The idea that time may vary from place to place is a difficult one, but it is the idea Einstein used, and it is correct – believe it or not.   Richard P. Feynman

Richard P. Feynman

I do not envy people who think they have a complete explanation of the world, for the simple reason that they are obviously wrong.   Salman Rushdie

Salman Rushdie

The whole history of physics proves that a new discovery is quite likely lurking at the next decimal place.   Floyd K. Richtmeyer

It would be a poor thing to be an atom in a universe without physicists, and physicists are made of atoms. A physicist is an atom's way of knowing about atoms.
George Wald

The task of asking nonliving matter to speak and the responsibility for interpreting its reply is that of physics.

Julius Thomas Fraser

In physics, you don't have to go around making trouble for yourself – nature does it for you.

Frank Wilczek

Reason, Observation, and Experience – the Holy Trinity of Science.

Robert G. Ingersoll

In speaking of the energy of the field, however, I wish to be understood literally. All energy is the same as mechanical energy, whether it exists in the form of motion or in that of elasticity, or in any other form. The energy in electromagnetic phenomena is mechanical energy.

James Clerk Maxwell

James Clerk Maxwell

Science is organised knowledge.

Herbert Spencer

Herbert Spencer

Science is the systematic quest for knowledge and understanding, whatever the topic, and wherever it leads.

Kathleen Erickson

Science is nothing but perception.   Plato

Plato

Man is the only creature endowed with the capacity to understand cosmic events
and to promote the rationality of Nature.   Origen of Alexandria

Origen of Alexandria

We are now certain that the world is not a deterministic mechanism. [commenting
on the mechanical universe à la Laplace]   Nick Herbert

Classical physics had its defects, experiments it could not explain, that eventually
led to its downfall. As far as we can tell, there is no experiment the quantum
theory does not explain, at least in principle.   Nick Herbert

Science is simply common sense at its best – that is, rigidly accurate in observation, and merciless to fallacy in logic.   Thomas Henry Huxley

Scientific principles and laws do not lie on the surface of nature. They are hidden, and must be wrested from nature by an active and elaborate technique of inquiry.
John Dewey

John Dewey

That deeply emotional conviction of the presence of a superior reasoning power, which is revealed in the incomprehensible universe, forms my idea of God.
Albert Einstein

God [could] vary the laws of Nature, and make worlds of several sorts in several parts of the universe. Sir Isaac Newton

It was not just the Church that resisted the heliocentrism of Nicolaus Copernicus.
Tycho Brahe

An experiment is a question which science poses to Nature, and a measurement is the recording of Nature's answer. Max Planck

Max Planck

Theories are not so much wrong as incomplete.   Isaac Asimov

A scientist tells himself a story and then finds out by experiment whether it is true or not.   Albert Einstein

Albert Einstein

The hypotheses we accept ought to explain phenomena which we have observed. But they ought to do more than this: our hypotheses ought to *foretell* phenomena which have not yet been observed.   William Whewell

The chess-board is the world; the pieces are the phenomena of the universe; the rules of the game are what we call the laws of Nature. The player on the other side is hidden from us. We know that his play is always fair, and patient. But also we know, to our cost, that he never overlooks a mistake, or makes the smallest allowance for ignorance.   Thomas Henry Huxley

Einstein, twenty-six years old, only three years away from crude privation, still a patent examiner, published in the Annalen der Physik in 1905 five papers on entirely different subjects. Three of them were among the greatest in the history of physics. One, very simple, gave the quantum explanation of the photoelectric effect – it was this work for which, sixteen years later, he was awarded the Nobel prize. Another dealt with the phenomenon of Brownian motion, the apparently erratic movement of tiny particles suspended in a liquid: Einstein showed that these movements satisfied a clear statistical law. This was like a conjuring trick, easy when explained: before it, decent scientists could still doubt the concrete existence of atoms and molecules: this paper was as near direct proof of their concreteness as a theoretician could give. The third paper was the special theory of relativity, which quietly amalgamated space, time and matter into one fundamental unity. This last paper contains no references and quotes no authority. All of them are written in a style unlike any other theoretical physicist's. They contain very little mathematics. There is a good deal of verbal commentary. The conclusions, the bizarre conclusions, emerge as though with the greatest of ease: the reasoning is unbreakable. It looks as though he had reached the conclusions by pure thought, unaided, without listening to the opinions of others. To a surprisingly large extent, that is precisely what he had done. It is pretty safe to say that, so long as physics lasts, no one will again hack out three major breakthroughs in one year.

Sir Charles Percy Snow

Quantum mechanics has explained all of chemistry and most of physics.

Paul Adrien Maurice Dirac

Paul Adrien Maurice Dirac

But are we sure of our observational facts? Scientific men are rather fond of saying pontifically that one ought to be quite sure of one's observational facts before embarking on theory. Fortunately those who give this advice do not practice what they preach. Observation and theory get on best when they are mixed together, both helping one another in the pursuit of truth. It is a good rule not to put overmuch confidence in a theory until it has been confirmed by observation. I hope I shall not shock the experimental physicists too much if I add that it is also a good rule not to put overmuch confidence in the observational results that are put forward until they have been confirmed by theory.   Sir Arthur Stanley Eddington

Sir Arthur Eddington

Odd how the creative power at once brings the whole universe to order.

Virginia Woolf

Virginia Woolf

Scientists speak of the law of inertia or the Second Law of Thermodynamics as if some great legislative in the sky once met and set down the rules to govern the universe.   Victor J. Stenger

In answer to the question of why it happened, I offer the modest proposal that our universe is simply one of those things which happen from time to time.

Edward P. Tryon

The crux ... is that the vast majority of the mass of the universe seems to be missing.   William J. Broad

Scientists were rated as great heretics by the church, but they were truly religious men because of their faith in the orderliness of the universe.   Albert Einstein

Now, my own suspicion is that the universe is not only queerer than we suppose, but queerer than we can suppose. I have read and heard many attempts at a systematic account of it, from materialism and theosophy to the Christian system or that of Kant, and I have always felt that they were much too simple. I suspect that there are more things in heaven and earth that are dreamed of, or can be dreamed of, in any philosophy. That is the reason why I have no philosophy myself, and must be my excuse for dreaming.   John Burden Sanderson Haldane

If I have ever made any valuable discoveries, it has been owing more to patient attention, than to any other talent.   Sir Isaac Newton

From a consideration of the immense volume of newly discovered facts in the field of physics, especially atomic physics, in recent years it might well appear to the layman that the main problems were already solved and that only more detailed work was necessary.   Victor Francis Hess

Victor Francis Hess

Whoever has undergone the intense experience of successful advances made in [science], is moved by profound reverence for the rationality made manifest in existence.   Sir Isaac Newton

Give me a firm place to stand and I will move the Earth.   Archimedes

Newton's cosmology is very easy to understand and very hard to believe.

Alfred North Whitehead

[Max Planck] was one of the finest people I have ever known ... but he really didn't understand physics, [because] during the eclipse of 1919 he stayed up all night to see if it would confirm the bending of light by the gravitational field. If he had really understood [general relativity], he would have gone to bed the way I did.   Albert Einstein

Absolute, true, and mathematical time, of itself, and from its own nature, flows equably without relation to anything external, and by another name is called duration: relative, apparent, and common time, is some sensible and external ... measure of duration by means of motion, which is used instead of true time; such as an hour, a day, a month, a year.   Sir Isaac Newton

When forced to summarise the general theory of relativity in one sentence: Time and space and gravitation have no separate existence from matter.

Albert Einstein

From henceforth, space by itself, and time by itself, have vanished into the merest
shadows and only a kind of blend of the two exists in its own right.

Hermann Minkowski

Hermann Minkowski

For every one billion particles of antimatter there were one billion and one particles of matter. And when the mutual annihilation was complete, one billionth
remained – and that's our present universe.   Albert Einstein

Some physicists thought that it might even become necessary to give up the conservation laws in their current form, especially in connection with the problem of
beta decay.   J. Hans D. Jensen

J. Hans D. Jensen

I have done a terrible thing: I have postulated a particle that cannot be detected.
[Wolfgang Pauli (after postulating the existence of the neutrino, a particle with no
mass and no electric charge, in order to save the law of energy conservation.)]

Wolfgang Pauli

The connection between symmetries and conservation laws is one of the great discoveries of twentieth century physics. But I think very few non-experts will have heard either of it or its maker – Emily Noether, a great German mathematician. But it is as essential to twentieth century physics as famous ideas like the impossibility of exceeding the speed of light.
Lee Smolin

There is geometry in the humming of the strings, there is music in the spacing of the spheres.
Pythagoras

Pythagoras

As long as algebra and geometry have been separated, their progress has been slow and their uses limited; but when these two sciences have been united, they have lent each mutual forces, and have marched together towards perfection.
Joseph-Louis Lagrange

Joseph-Louis Lagrange

The black holes of nature are the most perfect macroscopic objects there are in the universe: the only elements in their construction are our concepts of space and time.   Subrahmanyan Chandrasekhar

Evolutionary cosmology formulates theories in which a universe is capable of giving rise to and generating future universes out of itself, within black holes or whatever.   Robert Nozick

Famous last words: 'what a lovely black hole.'   Sir Arnold Wolfendale

Sir Arnold Wolfendale

No point is more central than this, that empty space is not empty. It is the seat of the most violent physics.   John Archibald Wheeler

Space, and space again, is the infinite deity which surrounds us and in which we are ourselves contained.   Max Beckmann

You cannot have an elliptical orbit that passes through the Schwarzschild radius. I mean, more than once.   Paul Lutus

In effect, we have redefined the task of science to be the discovery of laws that will enable us to predict events up to the limits set by the uncertainty principle.
                                                                      Stephen W. Hawking

The effort to understand the universe is one of the very few things that lifts human life a little above the level of farce, and gives it some of the grace of tragedy.
                                                                      Steven Weinberg

The celestial order and the beauty of the universe compel me to admit that there is some excellent and eternal being, who deserves the respect and homage of man.
                                                                      Cicero

The diversity of the phenomena of nature is so great, and the treasures hidden in the heavens so rich, precisely in order that the human mind shall never be lacking in fresh nourishment.					Johannes Kepler

Johannes Kepler

Spacetime grips mass, telling it how to move, and mass grips spacetime, telling it how to curve.					John Archibald Wheeler

The laws of nature are but the mathematical thoughts of God.					Euclid

Euclid

It is impossible to imagine the universe run by a wise, just and omnipotent God, but it is quite easy to imagine it run by a board of gods. If such a board actually exists it operates precisely like the board of a corporation that is losing money.					Henry Louis Mencken

Cosmologists are often in error, but never in doubt.					Yakov Borisovich Zel'dovich

God created two acts of folly. First, he created the Universe in a Big Bang. Second, He was negligent enough to leave behind evidence for this act in the form of the microwave radiation.   Paul Erdös

A letter Lemaître wrote to Nature magazine in 1931 was effectively the charter of what was to become the Big Bang theory. He theorised that this primordial explosion, occurring on 'a day without yesterday,' had burst forth from an extremely dense point of space and time. He began calling this the 'primeval atom.' By now Lemaître had become a celebrity in his own right for his revolutionary ideas. At an immense gathering of the British Association for the Advancement of Science in London the same year, he speculated before an audience of several thousand scientists that the cosmic rays may have originated in the primordial explosion. Eventually, he thought, they might prove to be material evidence of the universe's 'natural beginning.'   John C. Mather, John Irvan Boslough

Tune your television to any channel it doesn't receive, and about 1 percent of the dancing static you see is accounted for by this ancient remnant of the Big Bang. The next time you complain that there is nothing on, remember that you can always watch the birth of the universe.   Bill Bryson

The universe is one of God's thoughts.   Friedrich Schiller

Friedrich Schiller

The chief aim of all investigations of the external world should be to discover the rational order and harmony which has been imposed on it by God and which He revealed to us in the language of mathematics.   Johannes Kepler

It is a mathematical fact that the casting of this pebble from my hand alters the centre of gravity of the Universe.   Thomas Carlyle

The centre of the universe is everywhere, and the circumference nowhere.

Giordano Bruno

As we shall see, the concept of time has no meaning before the beginning of the universe. This was first pointed out by St. Augustine. When asked: What did God do before he created the universe? Augustine didn't reply: He was preparing Hell for people who asked such questions. Instead, he said that time was a property of the universe that God created, and that time did not exist before the beginning of the universe.

Stephen W. Hawking

One does not have to appeal to God to set the initial conditions for the creation of the universe, but if one does He would have to act through the laws of physics.

Stephen W. Hawking

Einstein's equations do not specify the universe; rather they may be considered a general framework within which you can construct many different model universes.

Tony Rothman

At rest, however, in the middle of everything is the Sun.   Nicolaus Copernicus

In the centre of everything rules the Sun; for who in this most beautiful temple could place this luminary at another better place whence it can light up the whole at once? In this arrangement we thus find an admirable harmony of the world, and a constant harmonious connection between the motion and the size of the orbits as could not be found otherwise.   Nicolaus Copernicus

Nicolaus Copernicus

Whether a man is on the Earth, or the Sun, or some other star, it will always seem to him that the position that he occupies is the motionless center, and that all other things are in motion.   Nicholas de Cusa

Venus is far too hellish of a world for life to exist on or below the planet's surface.
                                                                                              Leonard David

Birth of Venus, Sandro Botticelli

Sandro Botticelli

This universe is not hostile, or yet is it friendly. It is simply indifferent.
                                                                                              John H. Holmes

The universe seems neither benign nor hostile, merely indifferent.   Carl Sagan

What a wonderful and amazing scheme have we here of the magnificent vastness of the universe! So many suns, so many earths.   Christiaan Huygens

Even if I knew nothing of the atoms, I would venture to assert on the evidence of the celestial phenomena themselves, supported by many other arguments, that the universe was certainly not created for us by divine power: it is so full of imperfection.   Lucretius

Lucretius

The universe is the largest possible physics laboratory, able to produce conditions more extreme than those achieved with our accelerators.   John Ellis

Particle physics provides the framework in which fundamental issues in cosmology may be resolved, including the origin and dominance of matter in the universe.
                                                                                                       John Ellis

My present work concerns the problems connected with the theory of elementary particles, the theory of gravitation and cosmology and I shall be glad if I can manage to make some contribution to these important branches of science.
                                                                                                 Andrei Sakharov

Andrei Sakharov

How many seconds are there in a year? If I tell you there are 3.155×10^7, you won't even try to remember it. On the other hand, who could forget that, to within half a percent, pi seconds is a nanocentury.   Tom Duff [Bell Labs]

The universe contains the record of its past the way that sedimentary layers of rock contain the geological record of the Earth's past.   Heinz R. Pagels

The most incomprehensible fact about the Universe is that it is comprehensible.
                                                                  Albert Einstein

The Lord created the universe in seven days but the Lord had the wonderful advantage of being able to work alone.   Kofi Annan

Kofi Annan

There is no law governing all things.   Giordano Bruno

Giordano Bruno

Evolution, of course, is not something that simply applies to life here on earth; it applies to the whole universe.   John Polkinghorne

The laws of nature must have existed before even time began in order for the beginning to happen. We say this, we believe it, but can we prove it? No.
                                                                  Leon Lederman

Astronomy is perhaps the science whose discoveries owe least to chance, in which human understanding appears in its whole magnitude, and through which man can best learn how small he is.   Georg Christoph Lichtenberg

Georg Christoph Lichtenberg

Having probes in space is like having a cataract removed.   Hannes Alfvén

I don't pretend to understand the Universe – it's a great deal bigger than I am.
                                                                 Thomas Carlyle

I contemplated man's little spark, what it should be valued before God alongside of this great work of heaven and earth.   Jacob Böhme

Jacob Böhme

We live in a changing universe, and few things are changing faster than our conception of it.   Timothy Ferris

Celestial navigation is based on the premise that the Earth is the center of the universe. The premise is wrong, but the navigation works. An incorrect model can be a useful tool.   Kelvin Throop III

If the experience of science teaches anything, it's that the world is very strange and surprising. The many revolutions in science have certainly shown that.

John Polkinghorne

John Polkinghorne

The term 'Big Bang' was coined with derisive intent by Fred Hoyle, and its endurance testifies to Sir Fred's creativity and wit. Indeed, the term survived an international competition in which three judges – the television science reporter Hugh Downs, the astronomer Carl Sagan, and myself – sifted through 13,099 entries from 41 countries and concluded that none was apt enough to replace it. No winner was declared, and like it or not, we are stuck with 'Big Bang'.

Timothy Ferris

Ten or twenty billion years ago, something happened – the Big Bang, the event that began our universe. Why it happened is the greatest mystery we know. That it happened is reasonably clear. All the matter and energy now in the universe was concentrated at extremely high density – a kind of cosmic egg, reminiscent of the creation myths of many cultures – perhaps into a mathematical point with no dimensions at all. It was not that all the matter and energy were squeezed into a minor corner of the present universe; rather, the universe, matter and energy and the space they fill, occupied a very small volume. There was not much room for events to happen in.

Carl Sagan

In that titanic cosmic explosion, the universe began an expansion which has never ceased. It is misleading to describe the expansion of the universe as a sort of descending bubble viewed from the outside. By definition, nothing we can ever know about was outside. It is better to think of it from the inside, perhaps with grid-lines – imagined to adhere to the moving fabric of space – expanding uniformly in all directions. As space stretched, the matter and energy in the universe expanded with it rapidly and cooled. The radiation of the cosmic fireball, which, then as now, filled the universe, moved through the spectrum – from gamma rays to X rays to ultraviolet light; through the rainbow colors of the visible spectrum; into the infrared and radio regions. The remnants of that fireball, the cosmic background radiation, emanating from all parts of the sky can be detected by radio telescopes today. In the early universe, space was brilliantly illuminated. As time passed, the fabric of space continued to expand, the radiation cooled and, in ordinary visible light, for the first time space became dark, as it is today.

Carl Sagan

Where did all the matter and radiation in the universe come from in the first place? Recent intriguing theoretical research by physicists such as Steven Weinberg of Harvard and Ya.B. Zel'dovich in Moscow suggest that the universe began as a perfect vacuum and that all the particles of the material world were created from the expansion of space ...

William J. Kaufmann

Time is a fourth dimension, but distinctly different from the others in that it has a built-in arrow: we 'move' only towards the future.

Sir Martin Rees

We cannot predict what comes out of a singularity ... It is a disaster for science.

Stephen W. Hawking

Stephen W. Hawking

I don't think there is one unique real universe. ... Even the laws of physics themselves may be somewhat observer dependent.

Stephen W. Hawking

Philosophy is written in that great book which ever lies before our eyes. I mean the universe, but we cannot understand it if we do not first learn the language and grasp the symbols in which it is written. This book is written in the mathematical language, and the symbols are triangles, circles, and other geometrical figures, without whose help it is humanly impossible to comprehend a single word of it.

Galileo Galilei

If God created the world, his primary worry was certainly not to make its understanding easy for us.   Albert Einstein

I want to know how God created this world. I am not interested in this or that phenomenon, in the spectrum of this or that element. I want to know His thoughts; the rest are details.   Albert Einstein

When the solution is simple, God is answering.   Albert Einstein

Science cannot tell theology how to construct a doctrine of creation, but you can't construct a doctrine of creation without taking account of the age of the Universe and the evolutionary character of cosmic history.   John Polkinghorne

All the harmonies of creation find their resonance in man, the centre of the Universe.   Sergius Bulgakov

The universe is one but vast symbol of God.   Thomas Carlyle

I cannot believe that God plays dice with the cosmos.   Albert Einstein

Taken as a whole, the universe is absurd.   Walter Bagehot

Just as the letters of an alphabet can be variously ordered to create an infinite number of words, so diverse combinations of atoms produce an inexhaustible supply of entities.   Epicurus

Epicurus

Everything that occurs is the result of the atoms colliding, rebounding, and becoming entangled with one another, with no purpose or plan behind their motions.
                                                                        Epicurus

Order is manifestly maintained in the Universe ... governed by the sovereign will of God.   James Prescott Joule

James Prescott Joule

Of course, nobody would deny the importance of human beings for theological thinking, but the time span of history that theologians think about is a few thousand years of human culture rather than the fifteen billion years of the history of the universe.   John Polkinghorne

One world is enough.   Sting

I will no more believe that the universe was formed by a fortuitous concourse of atoms, than that the accidental jumbling of the alphabet would fall into a most ingenious treatise of philosophy.   Jonathan Swift

Jonathan Swift

Of the general theory of relativity you will be convinced, once you have studied it. Therefore, I am not going to defend it with a single word.   Albert Einstein

All art is an imitation of Nature.   Seneca

Seneca

If we are still here to witness the destruction of our planet some five billion years or more hence . . . , then we will have achieved something so unprecedented in the history of life that we should be willing to sing our swan song with joy.

Stephen Jay Gould

We have sought for firm ground and found none. The deeper we penetrate, the more restless becomes the universe; all is rushing about and vibrating in a wild dance.   Max Born

Classical physics has been superseded by quantum theory: quantum theory is verified by experiments. Experiments must be described in terms of classical physics.   Carl Friedrich von Weizsäcker

No language which lends itself to visualisability can describe quantum jumps.

Max Born

The whole visible universe is but a storehouse of images and signs to which the imagination will give a relative place and value; it is a sort of pasture which the imagination must digest and transform.   Charles Baudelaire

Charles Baudelaire

Mathematics: The alphabet God used to describe the universe.   Galileo Galilei

Galileo Galilei

Even if there is only one possible unified theory, it is just a set of rules and equations. What is it that breathes fire into the equations and makes a universe for them to describe? The usual approach of science of constructing a mathematical model cannot answer the questions of why there should be a universe for the model to describe. Why does the universe go to all the bother of existing? Is the unified theory so compelling that it brings about its own existence? Or does it need a creator, and, if so, does he have any other effect on the universe? And who created him? Up to now, most scientists have been too occupied with the development of new theories that describe what the universe is to ask the question why. On the other hand, the people whose business it is to ask why, the philosophers, have not been able to keep up with the advance of scientific theories. In the eighteenth century, philosophers considered the whole of human knowledge, including science, to be their field and discussed questions such as: Did the universe have a beginning? However, in the nineteenth and twentieth centuries, science became too technical and mathematical for the philosophers, or anyone else except a few specialists. Philosophers reduced the scope of their inquiries so much that Wittgenstein, the most famous philosopher of this century, said, "The sole remaining task for philosophy is the analysis of language." What a comedown from the great tradition of philosophy from Aristotle to Kant! However, if we do discover a complete theory, it should in time be understandable in broad principle by everyone, not just a few scientists. Then we shall all, philosophers, scientists, and just ordinary people, be able to take part in the discussion of the question of why it is that we and the universe exist. If we find the answer to that, it would be the ultimate triumph of human reason – for then we would know the mind of God.

Stephen W. Hawking

There is a theory which states that if ever anyone discovers exactly what the universe is for and why it is here, it will instantly disappear and be replaced by something even more bizarrely inexplicable. There is another theory which states that this has already happened.　　　　　　　　　　　　　　　Douglas Adams

Douglas Adams

According to classical relativistic theories of gravity, there is inevitably a physical singularity at the origin of Big Bang cosmological models. These results indicate that, in some sense, there is a serious incompleteness in these theories, since physical singularities should be avoided in all physically meaningful theories.

Roger Penrose

Indeterminacy in quantum mechanics only arises when you perform what is called 'making a measurement' and that involves magnifying an event from the quantum level to the classical level.　　　　　　　　　　　　　　　Roger Penrose

The problems of language here are really serious. We wish to speak in some way about the structure of the atoms. But we cannot speak about atoms in ordinary language.　　　　　　　　　　　　　　　Werner Heisenberg

In fact, our ordinary description of nature, and the idea of the exact laws, rests upon the assumption that it is possible to observe the phenomena without appreciably influencing them.　　　　　　　　　　　　　　　Werner Heisenberg

Mathematics, rightly viewed, possesses not only truth but supreme beauty – a beauty cold and austere, like that of a sculpture, without appeal to any part of our weaker nature, without the gorgeous trapping of painting or music, yet sublimely pure, and capable of a stern perfection such as only the greatest art can show. The true spirit of delight, the exaltation, the sense of being more than man, which is the touchstone of the highest excellence, is to be found in mathematics as surely as in poetry.　　　　　　　　　　　　　　　Bertrand A. W. Russell

One cannot escape the feeling that these mathematical formulas have an independent existence and an intelligence of their own, that they are wiser than we are, wiser even than their discoverers, that we get more out of them than was originally put into them.   Heinrich Rudolf Hertz

Heinrich Rudolf Hertz

A mathematical truth is timeless, it does not come into being when we discover it. Yet its discovery is a very real event, it may be an emotion like a great gift from a fairy.   Erwin Schrödinger

Mathematics is the only science where one never knows what one is talking about nor whether what is said is true.   Bertrand A. W. Russell

Bertrand A. W. Russell

I have declared infinite worlds to exist beside this our earth. It would not be worthy of God to manifest Himself in less than an infinite universe.   Giordano Bruno

Nothing new can be created in the Universe because of the infinity of elapsed time.   Plutarch

For the universe is infinite; now that which is infinite hath neither beginning nor limit, so it does not belong to it to possess a middle: for infinity is the deprivation of limits.   Plutarch

One may understand the cosmos, but never the ego; the self is more distant than any star.   Gilbert Keith Chesterton

Gilbert Keith Chesterton

The capabilities of humans are insufficient to understand the history and evolution of the Universe. It is totally in vain to try to construct a meaningful model of the cosmos from the insignificant human perspective.
                                          Johann Wolfgang von Goethe

Of the 'real' universe we know nothing, except that there exist as many versions of it as there are perceptive minds. Each man lives alone in his private universe.
                                                        Gerald Bullett

Duct tape is like the force. It has a light side, and a dark side, and it holds the universe together.   Carl Zwanzig

Everyone has his dark side and so does the universe.   Claus Grupen

The startling truth finally became apparent, and it was this: Numbers written on restaurant checks within the confines of restaurants do not follow the same mathematical laws as numbers written on any other pieces of paper in any other parts of the Universe. This single statement took the scientific world by storm. So many mathematical conferences got held in such good restaurants that many of the finest minds of a generation died of obesity and heart failure, and the science of mathematics was put back by years.   Douglas Adams

A vacuum is a hell of a lot better than some of the stuff that nature replaces it
with.   Tennessee Williams

Tennessee Williams

In the beginning the Universe was created. This has made a lot of people very
angry and been widely regarded as a bad move.   Douglas Adams

Everything you've learned in school as "obvious" becomes less and less obvious
as you begin to study the universe. For example, there are no solids in the universe.
There's not even a suggestion of a solid. There are no absolute continuums. There
are no surfaces. There are no straight lines.   Richard Buckminster Fuller

Praying is to ask that the laws of the universe be annulled on behalf of a single
petitioner confessedly unworthy.   Ambrose Bierce

Tell a man there are 300 billion stars in the universe and he'll believe you. Tell
him a bench has wet paint on it and he'll have to touch to be sure.   Anonymous

The most advantageous, pre-eminent thing thou canst do is not to exhibit nor
display thyself within the limits of our galaxy, but rather depart instantaneously
whence thou even now standest and flee to yet another rotten planet in the universe, if thou canst have the good fortune to find one.   Thomas Carlyle

The two most common things in the universe are hydrogen and stupidity.
                                                                       Harlan Ellison

We know next to nothing about virtually everything. It is not necessary to know
the origin of the universe; it is necessary to want to know. Civilization depends
not on any particular knowledge, but on the disposition to crave knowledge.
                                                                       George Will

The biggest difference between time and space is that you can't reuse time.

Merrick Furst

Had I been present at Creation, I would have given some useful hints for the better ordering of the Universe.   Alfonso the Wise; King of Castile

Mind and matter in our little speck of the universe are only two out of infinite varieties of existence which we are not competent to conceive – in the midst of which ... we might be set down, with no more notion of what was about us, than the worm in a flower-pot, on a London balcony has of the life of the great city ...   Thomas Henry Huxley

If you've done six impossible things before breakfast, why not round it off with dinner at Milliway's, the restaurant at the end of the universe.   Woody Allen

Woody Allen

Light brings us the news of the Universe.   Sir William Bragg

A grain of sand includes the universe.   Samuel Taylor Coleridge

The universe is full of magical things, patiently waiting for our wits to grow sharper.   Eden Phillpotts

The universe may be the ultimate free lunch.   Alan Guth

2.2 Life

I don't believe in natural science.   Kurt Gödel

There is more information available at our fingertips during a walk in the woods than in any computer system.   Mark Weiser

Representation of the world, like the world itself, is the work of men; they describe it from their own point of view, which they confuse with the absolute truth.
                                                              Simone de Beauvoir

Simone de Beauvoir

Either mathematics is too big for the human mind or the human mind is more than a machine.   Kurt Gödel

Kurt Gödel

The Analytical Engine weaves algebraic patterns, just as the Jacquard loom weaves flowers and leaves.   Ada Lovelace

The most exciting phrase to hear in science, the one that heralds the most discoveries, is not "Eureka!" (I found it!) but 'That's funny ...".   Isaac Asimov

A fact is a simple statement that everyone believes. It is innocent, unless found guilty. A hypothesis is a novel suggestion that no one wants to believe. It is guilty, until found effective.   Edward Teller

Veracity is the heart of morality.   Thomas Henry Huxley

Thomas Henry Huxley

A plurality should not be asserted without necessity.   William of Ockham

William of Ockham

Science is a wonderful thing if one does not have to earn one's living at it.
                                                            Albert Einstein

It is characteristic of science that the full explanations are often seized in their essence by the percipient scientist long in advance of any possible proof.
                                                            John Desmond Bernal

The scientist is not a person who gives the right answers, he's one who asks the right questions.   Claude Lévi-Strauss

Research is the process of going up alleys to see if they are blind.
                                                            Marston Bates

Science is the systematic classification of experience.   George Henry Lewes

Science when well digested is nothing but good sense and reason.
                                                                    Stanislaus, King of Poland

I have had my results for a long time: but I do not yet know how I am to arrive at
them.   Karl Friedrich Gauss

Karl Friedrich Gauss

It requires a very unusual mind to undertake the analysis of the obvious.
                                                                    Alfred North Whitehead

In all science, error precedes the truth, and it is better it should go first than last.
                                                                    Hugh Walpole

Science, my lad, is made up of mistakes, but they are mistakes which it is useful
to make, because they lead little by little to the truth.   Jules Verne

The essential point in science is not a complicated mathematical formalism or a
ritualised experimentation. Rather the heart of science is a kind of shrewd honesty
that springs from really wanting to know what the hell is going on!
                                                                    Nick Herbert

The important thing in science is not so much to obtain new facts as to discover
new ways of thinking about them.   Sir William Bragg

The effort to reconcile science and religion is almost always made, not by theologians, but by scientists unable to shake off altogether the piety absorbed with their
mother's milk.   Henry Louis Mencken

Search for the truth is the noblest occupation of man; its publication is a duty.

Madame de Staël

Science cannot solve the ultimate mystery of Nature. And it is because in the last analysis we ourselves are part of the mystery we are trying to solve.

Max Planck

A scientist in his laboratory is not a mere technician: he is also a child confronting natural phenomena that impress him as though they were fairy tales.

Marie Curie

Keep your eyes on the stars but keep your feet on the ground.

Theodore Roosevelt

Theodore Roosevelt

We are all in the gutter, but some of us are gazing at the stars.   Oscar Wilde

Oscar Wilde

No known roof is as beautiful as the skies above.   Michael O'Muircheartaigh

I know I can never look upon the stars without wondering why the whole world
does not become astronomers.   Thomas Wright of Durham

Thomas Wright of Durham

The saddest aspect of life right now is that science gathers knowledge faster than
society gathers wisdom.   Isaac Asimov

It has become appallingly obvious that our technology has exceeded our humanity.
Albert Einstein

It is now quite lawful for a Catholic woman to avoid pregnancy by a resort to
mathematics, though she is still forbidden to resort to physics and chemistry.
Henry Louis Mencken

We know very little, and yet it is astonishing that we know so much, and still more
astonishing that so little knowledge can give us so much power.
Bertrand A. W. Russell

Innocence about science is the worst crime today.   Sir Charles Percy Snow

Why are things as they are and not otherwise?   Johannes Kepler

All truths are easy to understand once they are discovered; the point is to discover
them.   Galileo Galilei

Once during a mass, Galileo in church
Conducted a major scientific search.
He measured with his pulse how a lamp did swing
That was to the ceiling tied with a string.
Varadaraja V. Raman

Don't become a mere recorder of facts, but try to penetrate the mystery of their origin.   Ivan Petrovitch Pavlov

Ivan Petrovitch Pavlov

To reach the source you must swim against the stream.   Confucius

Confucius

I do not know what I may appear to the world, but to myself I seem to have been only a boy playing on the sea-shore, and diverting myself in now and then finding a smoother pebble or a prettier shell than ordinary, whilst the great ocean of truth lay all undiscovered before me.   Sir Isaac Newton

The stellar universe is not so difficult of comprehension as the real actions of other people.   Marcel Proust

If intelligent life were common, there should have been colonisation by the inhabitants of planets around the many other stars which have come to the end of their lives. If the "people" leaving the other planets were similar to us, Earth would have seemed an appealing place to settle. But there is no evidence of their presence.   Sir Arnold Wolfendale

Life exists in the universe only because the carbon atom possesses certain exceptional properties. Sir James Jeans

It is an interesting problem, if one thinks one may have detected life elsewhere; how does one announce the results responsibly? Jocelyn Bell

Jocelyn Bell

If we are examples of anything in the cosmos, it is probably of magnificent mediocrity. Eric Chaisson

The religion that is afraid of science dishonors God and commits suicide.
Ralph Waldo Emerson

Ralph Waldo Emerson

I'm more interested in what I discover than what I invent.   Paul Simon

Paul Simon

A great pleasure in life is doing what people say you cannot do.

Walter Bagehot

I'm not at all certain that half a life is better than no life at all.   Ada Lovelace

A problem is a chance for you to do your best.   Duke Ellington

Duke Ellington

Make the best use of what is in your power, and take the rest as it happens.

Epictetus

Being a professional is doing the things you like to do on the days you don't feel
like doing them.   Julius Erving

The release of atomic energy has not created a new problem. It has merely made
more urgent the necessity of solving an existing one.   Albert Einstein

I am now almost certain that we need more radiation for better health.

John Cameron

We must not forget that when radium was discovered no one knew that it would prove useful in hospitals. Marie Curie

Marie Curie

It's ridiculous that time and time again we need a radioactive cloud coming out of a nuclear power station to remind us that atomic energy is extraordinarily danger-ous. Pierre Schaeffer

If I had not inherited a fortune I should probably not have cast my lot with math-ematics. Joseph-Louis Lagrange

The human mind always makes progress, but it is a progress in spirals. Madame de Staël

Madame de Staël

The investigation into the possible effects of cosmic rays on living organisms will also offer great interest. Victor Francis Hess

Victor Francis Hess

The smaller the hole, the clearer is the picture.
Abu Ali Al-Hasan Ibn Al-Haitham

Abu Ali Al-Hasan Ibn Al-Haitham

'Uncertainty' is NOT 'I don't know'. It is 'I can't know'. 'I am uncertain' DOES NOT mean 'I could be certain'. Werner Heisenberg

There are no physicists in the hottest part of hell, because the existence of a 'hottest part' implies a temperature difference, and any marginally competent physicist would immediately use this to run a heat engine and make some other part of hell comfortably cool. Richard Davisson

The whole problem with the world is that fools and fanatics are always so certain of themselves, but wiser people so full of doubts. Bertrand A. W. Russell

Whenever science makes a discovery, the devil grabs it while the angels are debating the best way to use it. Alan Valentine

Man, in his ignorance, supposed that all phenomena were produced by some intelligent powers, and with direct reference to him. Robert G. Ingersoll

Good art provokes emotion and thought. David Dory

Anyone who cannot cope with mathematics is not fully human. At best he is a tolerable subhuman who has learned to wear shoes, bathe, and not make messes in the house. Robert A. Heinlein
(also attributed to Lazarus Long)

Natural science does not simply describe and explain Nature; it is part of the interplay between Nature and ourselves. Werner Heisenberg

Werner Heisenberg

What we observe is not Nature itself, but Nature exposed to our method of questioning. Werner Heisenberg

In the cosmology that's behind psychology, there is no reason for anyone to be here or do anything. We are driven by the results of the Big Bang, billions of years ago, which eventually produced life, which eventually produced human beings. I'm an accident – a result – and therefore a victim. James Hillman

The point of view of a sinner is that the church promises him hell in the future, but cosmology proves that the glowing hell was in the past.

Yakov Borisovich Zel'dovich

According to the standard Big Bang theory the universe came into existence in a moment of infinite temperature and density some ten to fifteen billion years ago. Again and again when I have given a talk about the Big Bang theory someone in the audience during the question period has argued that the idea of a beginning is absurd; whatever moment we say saw the beginning of the Big Bang, there must have been a moment before that one. I have tried to explain that this is not necessarily so. It is true for instance that in our ordinary experience however cold it gets it is always possible for it to get colder, but there is such a thing as absolute zero; we cannot reach temperatures below absolute zero not because we are not sufficiently clever but because temperatures below absolute zero simply have no meaning. Stephen Hawking has offered what may be a better analogy; it makes sense to ask what is north of Austin or Cambridge or any other city, but it makes no sense to ask what is north of the North Pole.   Steven Weinberg

The only distinction between physicists and engineers is the physicists have more questions than answers while engineers have more answers than questions.

Anonymous

God created a number of possibilities in case some of his prototypes failed – that is the meaning of evolution.   Graham Greene

Graham Greene

I believe in God, only I spell it Nature.   Frank Lloyd Wright

Some call it Evolution and others call it God.   William H. Carruth

The science of today is the technology of tomorrow.   Edward Teller

A new scientific truth does not triumph by convincing its opponents and making them see the light, but rather because its opponents eventually die, and a new generation grows up that is familiar with it.   Max Planck

The most important thing in an argument, next to being right, is to leave an escape patch for your opponent, so that he can gracefully swing over to your side without too much apparent loss of face.   Sidney Harris

Physics is finished, young man. It's a dead-end street.   Max Planck's teacher

We live in a society exquisitely dependent on science and technology, in which hardly anyone knows anything about science and technology.   Carl Sagan

The Church says that the Earth is flat, but I know that it is round, for I have seen the shadow on the Moon, and I have more faith in a shadow than in the Church.
                                                                Ferdinand Magellan

I didn't think; I experimented.   Wilhelm Conrad Röntgen

Wilhelm Conrad Röntgen

There are no such things as applied sciences, only applications of science.
                                                                Louis Pasteur

More than any other time in history, mankind faces a crossroads. One path leads to despair and utter hopelessness. The other, to total extinction. Let us pray we have the wisdom to choose correctly.   Woody Allen

The aim of science is not to open the door to infinite wisdom, but to set a limit to infinite error.   Bertolt Brecht

As far as the laws of mathematics refer to reality, they are not certain, and as far as they are certain, they do not refer to reality.   Albert Einstein

If history has taught us one thing it is that, with hindsight, newly discovered laws always turn out to be quite logical extensions of what we have already known for a long time.   Gerald 't Hooft

All the effects of nature are only the mathematical consequence of a small number of immutable laws.   Pierre-Simon de Laplace

A law of geology, biology, or human psychology may stem from one or more amplified quantum events, each of which could have turned out differently. The amplifications can occur through a variety of mechanisms, including the phenomenon of chaos, which introduces, in certain situations, indefinitely large sensitivities of outcome to input.   Murray Gell-Mann

Second to agriculture, humbug is the biggest industry of our age.
                                                                        Alfred Nobel

Alfred Nobel

A theory should not consist only of words, but also of accurate mathematical rules for calculations.   Gerald 't Hooft

Translating mathematical formulae into plain language is sometimes impossible without a little cheating.   Gerald 't Hooft

Statistics are no substitute for judgment.   Henry Clay

Statistics will prove anything, even the truth. Noël Moynihan

Insisting on perfect safety is for people who don't have the balls to live in the real world. Mary Shaffer

There are some people that if they don't know, you can't tell them.
Louis Armstrong

Louis Armstrong

Now there is one outstandingly important fact regarding Spaceship Earth, and that is that no instruction book came with it. Richard Buckminster Fuller

What would life be if we had no courage to attempt anything?
Vincent van Gogh

Vincent van Gogh

Statistically, the probability of any one of us being here is so small that you'd think the mere fact of existing would keep us all in a contended dazzlement of surprise.   Lewis Thomas

Animals have these advantages over man; they never hear the clock strike, they die without any idea of death, they have no theologians to instruct them, their last moments are not disturbed by unwelcomed and unpleasant ceremonies, their funerals cost them nothing, and no one starts lawsuits over their wills.

Voltaire

Voltaire

The most technologically efficient machine that man ever invented is the book.

Northrop Frye

Your library is your paradise.   Erasmus of Rotterdam

Erasmus of Rotterdam

The best way to get great ideas is to get lots of ideas and throw the bad ones away.
Charles Thompson

If Edison had a needle to find in a haystack, he would proceed at once with the diligence of the bee to examine straw after straw until he found the object of his search. I was a sorry witness of such doings, knowing that a little theory and calculation would have saved him ninety per cent of his labor.   Nikola Tesla

Nikola Tesla

I never did a day's work in my life. It was all fun.   Thomas Alva Edison

The best way to show that a stick is crooked is not to argue about it, or spend your time trying to straighten it, but to lay a straight stick alongside of it.
Dwight L. Moody

Mathematics provides an invisible framework that molds the more visible surfaces of daily life.   Sheila Tobias

The paradox of our times is that as mathematics becomes increasingly powerful, only the powerful seem to benefit from it.   Sheila Tobias

There is no doubt that human survival will continue to depend more and more on human intellect and technology. It is idle to argue whether this is good or bad. The point of no return was passed long ago, before anyone knew it was happening.
Theodosius Dobzansky

You do not really understand something unless you can explain it to your grand-mother.   Albert Einstein

If it is 'well understood', query it.   Sir Arnold Wolfendale

Telling someone something he does not understand is pointless, even if you add
that he will not be able to understand it.   Ludwig Wittgenstein

I never am really satisfied that I understand anything; because, understand it well
as I may, my comprehension can only be an infinitesimal fraction of all I want to
understand about the many connections and relations which occur to me, how the
matter in question was first thought of or arrived at, etc., etc.   Ada Lovelace

Ada Lovelace

The hardest part of science is to know what question you are asking.
                                              Laura Maria Caterina Bassi Verati

Laura Maria Caterina Bassi Verati

A hundred times every day I remind myself that my inner and outer life depend
on the labours of other men, living and dead, and that I must exert myself in order
to give in the same measure as I have received.   Albert Einstein

If we do not permit the Earth to produce beauty and joy, it will not produce food
either.
                                                                    Joseph Krutch

Results! Why, man, I have gotten a lot of results. I know several thousand things
that don't work.
                                                               Thomas Alva Edison

The Sun, the Moon and the stars would all have disappeared years ago, had they
happened to be within the reach of predatory human hands.   Havelock Ellis

Fermi devoted a great deal of his time to the graduate students ... his teaching was
exemplary, minutely prepared, clear, with emphasis on simplicity and understanding of the basic ideas, rather than generalities and complications ... We would
knock at his office door, and if free, he would take us in, and then he would be
ours until the question was resolved.
                                                              Jack Steinberger

It is not difficult to teach Noether's theorem, as it is called; there is a beautiful
and intuitive idea behind it. I've explained it every time I've taught introductory
physics. But no textbook at this level mentions it. And without it one does not
really understand why the world is such that riding a bicycle is safe.
                                                                    Lee Smolin

It takes so long to train a physicist to the place where he understands the nature of
physical problems that he is already too old to solve them.
                                                           Eugene Paul Wigner

Decisiveness is often the art of timely cruelty.   Henri Antoine Becquerel

Henri Antoine Becquerel

All I know about the becquerel is that, like the Italian lira, you need an awful lot
to amount to very much.
                                                                   Arnold Allen

Every difficulty slurred over will be a ghost to disturb your repose later on.

Frédéric Chopin
(also attributed to Rabindranath Tagore)

Physicists just want to know what the world is made of, what are the smallest particles, and how they behave. Therefore they are always ahead of practical applications.   Otto Frisch

Otto Frisch

I'm not an expert in physics or cosmology or any of these matters, but the more we discover about how the world works the more we see these unpatterned patterns – all these orbits and orders and, within them, these variations.   Paul Muldoon

I recognise that many physicists are smarter than I am – most of them theoretical physicists. A lot of smart people have gone into theoretical physics, therefore the field is extremely competitive. I console myself with the thought that although they may be smarter and may be deeper thinkers than I am, I have broader interests than they have.   Linus Pauling

Of course, Einstein was a very great scientist indeed, and I have enormous respect for him, and great admiration for the discoveries he made. But he was very committed to a view of the objectivity of the physical world.   John Polkinghorne

Perhaps you can suggest some fantastic explanation. We understand that uranium really can't break up into barium. So try and think of some other possibility. Barium isotopes with much higher atomic weights than 137? If you can think of anything that might be publishable, then the three of us [Hahn, Meitner and Strassmann] would be together in this work after all. [In a letter to Lise Meitner]

Otto Hahn

It must certainly be a great joy for you and Strassmann that you have made the whole world of physics excited. That is really wonderful! [To Otto Hahn]

Lise Meitner

Lise Meitner

It is conceivable that when heavy nuclei are bombarded with neutrons these nuclei could break down into several fairly large fragments, which are certainly isotopes of known elements, but not neighbours of the irradiated elements. [In 1934]

Ida Noddack

Ida Noddack

Quantum theory is bizarre. In order to try and understand it we need to forget
everything we know about cause and effect, reality, certainty, and much else be-
sides. This is a different world, it has its own rules, rules of probability that make
no sense in our everyday world.   Richard P. Feynman

Quantum mechanics is very impressive. But an inner voice tells me that it is not
yet the real thing. The theory produces a good deal but hardly brings us closer
to the secret of the Old One. I am at all events convinced that He does not play
dice.   Albert Einstein

Quantum theory also tells us that the world is not simply objective; somehow it's
something more subtle than that. In some sense it is veiled from us, but it has a
structure that we can understand.   John Polkinghorne

The physical fabric of the world had to be such as to enable that ten billion year
preliminary evolution to produce the raw materials of life. Without it there would
not have been the chemical materials to allow life to evolve here on Earth.
                                                            John Polkinghorne

It is nice to know that the computer understands the problem. But I would like to
understand it too.   Eugene Paul Wigner

Eugene Paul Wigner

Even when all the possible scientific questions have been answered, the problems
of life remain completely untouched.   Ludwig Wittgenstein

Life is the art of drawing sufficient conclusions from insufficient premises.
                                                            Samuel Butler

I don't know why we are here, but I'm pretty sure that it is not in order to enjoy
ourselves.   Ludwig Wittgenstein

Indulge yourself in pleasures only in so far as they are necessary for the preservation of health.   Baruch Spinoza

Entia non sunt multiplicanda preater necessitatem. (We must not assume the existence of any entity until we are forced to do so.)   William of Ockham

There are no passengers on Spaceship Earth. We are all crew.
                                                                Marshall McLuhan

In this Theory of Everything, I have one major rule: Everybody is right. More specifically, everybody – including me – has some important pieces of truth, and all of those pieces need to be honored, cherished, and included in a more gracious, spacious, and compassionate embrace, a genuine T.O.E.   Ken Wilber

Exposing students to the history of science may not always make them friends of science, but the exposure offers a better basis for decision than fear or ignorance. In order to survive, mankind cannot know too much.   William R. Shea

Propose to any Englishman any principle or instrument, however admirable, and you will observe that the whole effort of the English mind is directed to find a difficulty, a defect, or an impossibility in it.   Charles Babbage

Charles Babbage

I am proud of the fact that I never invented weapons to kill.
                                                            Thomas Alva Edison

The precise statement of any problem is the most important step in its solution.
                                                                Edwin Bliss

For a successful technology, reality must take precedence over public relations, for nature cannot be fooled.   Richard P. Feynman

The idea that we shall be welcomed as new members into the galactic community is as unlikely as the idea that the oyster will be welcomed as a new member into the human community. We're probably not even edible.   John Ball

Obstacles are what you see when you take your eyes off the goal line.
                                                        Vince Lombardi

Whoever, in the pursuit of science, seeks after immediate practical utility may rest assured that he seeks in vain.   Hermann Ludwig Ferdinand von Helmholtz

It is folly to use as one's guide in the selection of fundamental science the criterion of utility. Not because (scientists) ... despise utility. But because ... useful outcomes are best identified after the making of discoveries, rather than before. [Concerning the allocation of research funds]   John C. Polanyi

Nothing tends so much to the advancement of knowledge as the application of a new instrument. The native intellectual powers of men in different times are not so much the causes of the different success of their labours, as the peculiar nature of the means and artificial resources in their possession.   Sir Humphry Davy

Perplexity is the beginning of knowledge.   Kahlil Gibran

Kahlil Gibran

Growing old is like being increasingly penalised for a crime you haven't committed.   Anthony Powell

There is more to life than increasing its speed.   Mahatma Gandhi

Growth for the sake of growth is the ideology of the cancer cell.

Edward Abbey

Available energy is the main object at stake in the struggle for existence and the evolution of the world.   Ludwig Boltzmann

Ludwig Boltzmann

All great things are simple, and many can be expressed in single words: freedom, justice, honor, duty, mercy, hope.   Sir Winston Churchill

Man had always assumed that he was more intelligent than dolphins because he had achieved so much ... the wheel, New York, wars, and so on, whilst all the dolphins had ever done was muck about in the water having a good time. But conversely the dolphins believed themselves to be more intelligent than man for precisely the same reasons.   Douglas Adams

Because things are the way they are, things will not stay the way they are.

Bertolt Brecht

Bertolt Brecht

Life is an unfoldment, and the further we travel the more truth we can comprehend. To understand the things that are at our door is the best preparation for understanding those that lie beyond.   Hypatia

Hypatia

Equations are more important to me, because politics is for the present, but an equation is something for eternity.   Albert Einstein

It is a good morning exercise for a research scientist to discard a pet hypothesis every day before breakfast.   Konrad Lorenz

To invent, you need a good imagination and a pile of junk.
                                    Thomas Alva Edison

No amount of skillful invention can replace the essential element of imagination.
                                    Edward Hopper

Edward Hopper

Science becomes dangerous only when it imagines that it has reached its goal.
George Bernard Shaw

Associate with men of good quality if you esteem your own reputation; for it is better to be alone than in bad company.
George Washington

George Washington

Nothing is more difficult and nothing requires more character than to find oneself in open opposition to one's time (and those one loves) and to say loudly: No!
Kurt Tucholsky

Kurt Tucholsky

Men who wish to know about the world must learn about it in its particular details.
Heraclitus of Ephesus

In science one tries to tell people, in such a way as to be understood by everyone, something that no one ever knew before. But in poetry, it's the exact opposite.
Paul Adrien Maurice Dirac

Science is the labor and handicraft of the mind; poetry can only be considered its recreation.
Francis Bacon

Historians have concluded that W. Heisenberg must have been contemplating his love life when he discovered the Uncertainty Principle: – when he had the time, de didn't have the energy and, – when the moment was right, he couldn't figure out the position.
Tryggvi Emilsson

When you reach the end of your rope, tie a knot in it and hang on.
Thomas Jefferson

It is easier to denature plutonium than to denature the evil spirit of man.
Albert Einstein

Great spirits have often encountered violent opposition from mediocre minds.
Albert Einstein

Everything that you could possibly imagine, you will find that Nature has been there before you.
John Berrill

What is now proved was once only imagined.
William Blake

An extremely healthy dose of skepticism about the reliability of science is an absolutely inevitable consequence of any scientific study of its track record.
Michael Scriven

No man has a good enough memory to be a successful liar.   Abraham Lincoln

Some scientists find, or so it seems, that they get their best ideas when smoking; others by drinking coffee or whiskey. Thus there is no reason why I should not admit that some may get their ideas by observing or by repeating observations.
Sir Karl Popper

Sir Karl Popper

Basic research may seem very expensive. I am a well-paid scientist. My hourly wage is equal to that of a plumber, but sometimes my research remains barren of results for weeks, months or years and my conscience begins to bother me for wasting the taxpayer's money. But in reviewing my life's work, I have to think that the expense was not wasted. Basic research, to which we owe everything, is relatively very cheap when compared with other outlays of modern society. The other day I made a rough calculation which led me to the conclusion that if one were to add up all the money ever spent by man on basic research, one would find it to be just about equal to the money spent by the Pentagon this past year.

Albert Szent-Györgyi

We have lost the art of living; and in the most important science of all, the science of daily life, the science of behavior, we are complete ignoramuses. We have psychology instead. David Herbert Lawrence

David Herbert Lawrence

Modern psychology takes completely for granted that behavior and neural function are perfectly correlated, that one is completely caused by the other. There is no separate soul or lifeforce to stick a finger into the brain now and then and make neural cells do what they would not otherwise. Actually, of course, this is a working assumption only. ... It is quite conceivable that someday the assumption will have to be rejected. But it is important also to see that we have not reached that day yet: the working assumption is a necessary one and there is no real evidence opposed to it. Our failure to solve a problem so far does not make it insoluble. One cannot logically be a determinist in physics and biology, and a mystic in psychology. Donald O. Hebb

There are only two ways to live your life. One is as though nothing is a miracle. The other is as though everything is a miracle. Albert Einstein

To climb steep hills requires slow pace at first.   Henry the Eighth

King Henry the Eighth

I like pigs. Dogs look up to us. Cats look down on us. Pigs treat us as equals.
                                                      Sir Winston Churchill

Sir Winston Churchill

We are dismayed when we find that even disaster cannot cure us of our faults.
                                                              Vauvenargues

Nothing is more responsible for the good old days than a bad memory.
                                                        Franklin P. Adams

Nothing happens to you that hasn't happened to someone else.
                                                          William Feather

Most people do not really want freedom, because freedom involves responsibility,
and most people are frightened of responsibility.   Sigmund Freud

Anyone can hold the helm when the sea is calm.   Publius Syrus

Television is actually closer to reality than anything in books. The madness of TV is the madness of human life. Camille Paglia

Camille Paglia

Drama is life with the dull bits cut out. Alfred Hitchcock

Alfred Hitchcock

Nobody, as long as he moves about among the chaotic currents of life, is without trouble. Carl Gustav Jung

Let us endeavour so to live that when we come to die even the undertaker will be sorry. Mark Twain

For fast acting relief, try slowing down. Lily Tomlin

He who hurries loses his time. Anonymous

With luck on your side, you can do without brains. Giordano Bruno

The reason so many people never get anywhere in life is because, when opportunity knocks, they are out in the backyard looking for four-leaf clovers.

Walter Chrysler

If something bad happens, you drink in order to forget; if something good happens, you drink in order to celebrate; and if nothing happens, you drink in order to make something happen.   Charles Bukowski

Charles Bukowski

Drowning your sorrows only irrigates them.   Ken Alstad

Life is full of disappointments; as one reaches one ridge there is always another and a higher one beyond which blocks the view.   Fridtjof Nansen

Fridtjof Nansen

I read about an Eskimo hunter who asked the local missionary priest, 'If I did not know about God and sin, would I go to hell?' 'No', said the priest, 'not if you did not know.' 'Then why', asked the Eskimo, 'did you tell me?'   Annie Dillard

Thus, the task is, not so much to see what no one has yet seen; but to think what nobody has yet thought, about that which everybody sees.   Erwin Schrödinger

In the practice of tolerance, one's enemy is the best teacher.   Dalai Lama

I wished to go completely outside and to make a symbolic start for my enterprise of regenerating the life of humankind within the body of society and to prepare a positive future in this context.   Joseph Beuys

Joseph Beuys

The future belongs to those who prepare for it today.   Malcolm X

Malcolm X

The meeting of two personalities is like the contact of two chemical substances: if there is any reaction, both are transformed.   Carl Gustav Jung

A university is what a college becomes when the faculty loses interest in students.   John Ciardi

A university without students is like an ointment without a fly.
                            Ed Nather [professor of astronomy at UT Austin]

A corporation is organized as a system – it has this department, that department,
that department ... they don't have any meaning separately; they only can function together. And also the body is a system. Society is a system in some sense.
And so on.   David Bohm

There is no likelihood man can ever tap the power of the atom.
                                                          Robert Millikan

You cannot have a science without measurement.   Richard W. Hamming

Science is facts; just as houses are made of stones, so is science made of facts; but
a pile of stones is not a house and a collection of facts is not necessarily science.
                                                     Jules Henri Poincaré

Let your life lightly dance on the edges of Time like dew on the tip of a leaf.
                                                    Rabindranath Tagore

All journeys have secret destinations of which the traveler is unaware.
                                                           Martin Buber

Martin Buber

There are three principles in a man's being and life, the principle of thought, the
principle of speech, and the principle of action. The origin of all conflict between
me and my fellow-men is that I do not say what I mean and I don't do what I
say.   Martin Buber

Insanity: doing the same thing over and over again and expecting different results.
Albert Einstein

A thief believes everybody steals.   Edgar Watson Howe

Edgar Watson Howe

2.3 Everything

Anyone who believes in science is ignoring the truth. Anonymous

Science is a differential equation. Religion is a boundary condition.
Alan M. Turing

We can only see a short distance ahead, but we can see plenty there that needs to be done. Alan M. Turing

Alan M. Turing

Observations always involve theory. Edwin Powell Hubble

Learning is ever in the freshness of its youth, even for the old. Aeschylus

Neutrino physics is largely an art of learning a great deal by observing nothing.
Haim Harari

[On the naming of the neutrino in 1934] ... one of the students asked whether the 'Chadwick neutron' was the same 'neutron' proposed by Pauli for the phenomena of beta transformation. "No," answered Fermi, il neutrone di Pauli è molto piú piccolo, cio è un neutrino." The name stuck ... George Gamow

If they succeed in making neutrinos, perhaps even in developing industrial applications of them, I suppose I shall have to believe in neutrinos – though I may feel that they have not been playing quite fair. Sir Arthur Eddington

The neutrino is about as close to intangibility as we can get in this world – the human soul, perhaps is the next stage. Anonymous

Neutrinos, they are very small
They have no charge and have no mass
And do not interact at all.

John Updike

John Updike

All science is either physics or stamp collecting. Sir Ernest Rutherford

You know, there's a right and wrong way to do everything.
Arthur Stanley Jefferson and Oliver Norvell Hardy

A hair divides what is false and true. Omar Al-Khayyam

A task slowly done is surely done.
Arthur Stanley Jefferson and Oliver Norvell Hardy

Arthur Stanley Jefferson and Oliver Norvell Hardy

A comedian does funny things. A good comedian does things funny.
Buster Keaton

Think slow, act fast.   Buster Keaton

Buster Keaton

What one writer can make in the solitude of one room is something no power can
easily destroy.   Salman Rushdie

Truth is stranger than fiction, but it is because fiction is obliged to stick to possibilities; truth isn't.   Mark Twain

Mark Twain

DNA was the first three-dimensional Xerox machine.   Kenneth Boulding

I think physicists are the Peter Pans of the human race. They never grow up, and
they keep their curiosity.   Isidor Isaac Rabi

People often say that I'm curious about too many things at once ... But can you
really forbid a man from harbouring a desire to know and embrace everything that
surrounds him?   Alexander von Humboldt

In theory, there is no difference between theory and practice. But, in practice, there is.   Jan L. A. van de Snepscheut

We may brave human laws, but we cannot resist natural ones.   Jules Verne

Jules Verne

A visitor to Niels Bohr's country cottage asked him about a horseshoe nailed above the front door. 'Surely, Professor Bohr, you do not really believe that a horseshoe over the entrance to a home brings good luck?' 'No,' answered Bohr, 'I certainly do not believe in this superstition. But you know,' he added, 'they say it brings luck even if you don't believe in it.'   Nick Herbert

Quantum theory is like Bohr's horseshoe: it works no matter what a person believes.   Nick Herbert

Science commits suicide when it adopts a creed.   Thomas Henry Huxley

Science is the great antidote to the poison of enthusiasm and superstition.
                                                              Adam Smith

Science, in the very act of solving problems, creates more of them.
                                                          Abraham Flexner

Science is always wrong. It never solves a problem without creating ten more.
                                                      George Bernard Shaw

There is no national science just as there is no national multiplication table; what is national is no longer science.   Anton Chekhov

We live in a world that is governed by Einstein's physics and Frankenstein's logic.
Bertrand A. W. Russell

We own the world, that is the cosmos and our own constitution.
Oswald von Nell-Breuning

The power of accurate observation is commonly called cynicism by those who have not got it.   George Bernard Shaw

George Bernard Shaw

Inanimate objects can be classified scientifically into three major categories; those that don't work, those that break down and those that get lost.   Russell Baker

"Your Highness, I have no need of this hypothesis." [in reply to Napoleon on why his works on celestial mechanics make no mention of God]
Pierre Simon de Laplace

Pierre Simon de Laplace

One ought to be ashamed to make use of the wonders of science embodied in a radio set, while appreciating them as little as a cow appreciates the botanical marvels in the plant she munches. Albert Einstein

If it weren't for electricity we'd all be watching television by candlelight.
George Gobol

Electricity is of two kinds, positive and negative. The difference is, I presume, that one comes a little more expensive, but is more durable; the other is a cheaper thing, but the moths get into it. Stephen Leacock

Only divine love bestows the keys of knowledge. Arthur Rimbaud

Arthur Rimbaud

The intense focusing on a very tiny field is not difficult if you like it genuinely.
Jack Steinberger

Jack Steinberger

There is no adequate defense, except stupidity, against the impact of a new idea.

Percy Williams Bridgman

I can't understand why people are frightened of new ideas. I'm frightened of the old ones.

John Cage

John Cage

Insofar as mathematics is about reality, it is not certain, and insofar as it is certain, it is not about reality.

Albert Einstein

It is well known that geometry presupposes not only the concept of space but also the first fundamental notions for constructions in space as given in advance. It only gives nominal definitions for them, while the essential means of determining them appear in the form of axioms. The relationship of these presumptions is left in the dark; one sees neither whether and in how far their connection is necessary, nor a priori whether it is possible. From Euclid to Legendre, to name the most renowned of modern writers on geometry, this darkness has been lifted neither by the mathematicians nor the philosophers who have laboured upon it.

Bernhard Riemann

Bernhard Riemann

In every department of physical science there is only so much science, properly so-called, as there is mathematics.   Immanuel Kant

We believe in the possibility of a theory which is able to give a complete description of reality, the laws of which establish relations between the things themselves and not merely between their probabilities ... God does not play dice.
                                                                                        Albert Einstein

A mathematician may say anything he pleases, but a physicist must be at least partially true.   J. Willard Gibbs

If anybody says he can think about quantum problems without getting giddy, that only shows he has not understood the first thing about them.   Niels Bohr

A man must have a certain amount of intelligent ignorance to get anywhere.
                                                                        Charles Franklin Kettering

The axiomatic basis of theoretical physics cannot be abstracted from experience, but must be freely invented. Experience may suggest the appropriate mathematical concepts, but they most certainly cannot be deduced from it.
                                                                                        Albert Einstein

Two seemingly incompatible conceptions can each represent an aspect of the truth ... They may serve in turn to represent the facts without ever entering into direct conflict.   Prince Louis de Broglie

Prince Louis de Broglie

It is a capital mistake to theorise before one has data. Insensibly one begins to twist facts to suit theories instead of theories to suit facts.

Sherlock Holmes, the fictional creation of Sir Arthur Conan Doyle

Errors using inadequate data are much less than those using no data at all.

Charles Babbage

It is as fatal as it is cowardly to blink facts because they are not to our taste.

John Tyndall

The production of useful work is strictly limited by the laws of thermodynamics. The production of useless work seems to be unlimited.   Donald E. Simanek

Introductory physics courses are taught at three levels: physics with calculus, physics without calculus, and physics without physics.   Anonymous

One thing that makes the adventure of working in our field particularly rewarding, especially in attempting to improve the theory, is that ... a chief criterion for the selection of a correct hypothesis ... seems to be the criterion of beauty, simplicity, or elegance.   Murray Gell-Mann

Physical laws should have mathematical beauty.   Paul Adrien Maurice Dirac

For me the greatest beauty always lies in the greatest clarity.

Gotthold Ephraim Lessing

Gotthold Ephraim Lessing

When I am working on a problem, I never think about beauty. I only think about how to solve the problem. But when I have finished, if the solution is not beautiful, I know it is wrong.   Richard Buckminster Fuller

If it looks wrong, it is wrong.   Sir Arnold Wolfendale

As a matter of fact, mathematics is a science, which requires a maximum of imagination.   Sofja Kowalewskaja

Sofja Kowalewskaja

Here arises a puzzle that has disturbed scientists of all periods. How is it possible that mathematics, a product of human thought that is independent of experience, fits so excellently the objects of physical reality? Can human reason without experience discover by pure thinking properties of real things?   Albert Einstein

We haven't the money, so we've got to think.   Sir Ernerst Rutherford

Physics isn't a religion. If it were, we'd have a much easier time raising money.
                                                          Leon Lederman

Leon Lederman

God used beautiful mathematics in creating the world.

Paul Adrien Maurice Dirac

Pick a flower on earth and you move the farthest star.

Paul Adrien Maurice Dirac

What can stars do? Nothing ... But sit on their axis!   Charlie Chaplin

All the physics you have learned so far is massless, frictionless, and pointless.

Minking K. Chyu

A mathematician is a machine for turning coffee into theorems.   Paul Erdös

Don't worry about your difficulties in mathematics; I can assure you that mine are still greater. [Einstein's reply to a schoolgirl, who had problems in mathematics]

Albert Einstein

When I was a child, the Earth was said to be two billion years old. Now scientists say it's four and a half billion. So that makes me two and a half billion.

Paul Erdös

This world, after all our science and sciences, is still a miracle; wonderful, inscrutable, magical and more, to whosoever will think of it.   Thomas Carlyle

Thomas Carlyle

The entire world is my temple, and a very fine one too, if I'm not mistaken, and I'll never lack priests to serve it as long as there are men.

Erasmus of Rotterdam

Science and art belong to the whole world, and the barriers of nationality vanish
before them.   Johann Wolfgang von Goethe

Only when genius is married to science, can the highest results be produced.
                                                                        Herbert Spencer

Any sufficiently advanced technology will be indistinguishable from magic.
                                                                        Arthur C. Clarke

No matter how wonderful our new technology is, we still have to clean it.
                                                                        Héloïse

Héloïse

Technology is a way of organizing the universe so that man doesn't have to experience it.   Max Frisch

OK, so what's the speed of dark?   Steven Wright

While you are experimenting, do not remain content with the surface of things.
                                                                Ivan Petrovitch Pavlov

Anyone who has never made a mistake has never tried anything new.
                                                                        Albert Einstein

A little inaccuracy sometimes saves a ton of explanation.
                                                                Hector Hugh Munro (Saki)

Anything becomes interesting if you look at it long enough.   Gustave Flaubert

Gustave Flaubert

You should never rest. Because in the moment when you stop to work, you think about yourself. And from this moment on you are sick, or you feel sick, which is essentially the same.   Gustave Flaubert

Science will stagnate if it is made to serve practical goals.   Albert Einstein

Happy is he who gets to know the reasons for things.   Virgil

The joy of discovery is certainly the liveliest that the mind of man can ever feel.
                                                              Claude Bernard

The real voyage of discovery consists not in seeking new landscapes but in having new eyes.   Marcel Proust

Marcel Proust

I think that if it had been a religion that first maintained the notion that all the matter in the entire universe had once been contained in an area smaller than the point of a pin, scientists probably would have laughed at the idea.

Marillyn vos Savant

The strongest arguments prove nothing so long as the conclusions are not verified by experience. Experimental science is the queen of sciences and the goal of all speculation.

Roger Bacon

All science is experiential; but all experience must be related back to and derives its validity from the conditions and context of consciousness in which it arises, i.e., the totality of our nature.

Wilhelm Dilthey

Wilhelm Dilthey

And thought struggles against the results, trying to avoid those unpleasant results while keeping on with that way of thinking. That is what I call 'sustained incoherence'.

David Bohm

David Bohm

It is not the possession of truth, but the success which attends the seeking after it, that enriches the seeker and brings happiness to him.   Max Planck

Truth in science can be defined as the working hypothesis best suited to open the way to the next better one.   Konrad Lorenz

All of physics is either impossible or trivial. It is impossible until you understand it, and then it becomes trivial.   Sir Ernest Rutherford

Nothing exists except atoms and empty space, everything else is opinion.
                    Democritus of Abdera

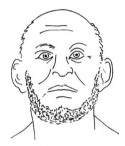

Democritus of Abdera

Bosons love to come together; fermions can't stand each other.
                    Daniel Kleppner

In these days, a man who says a thing cannot be done is quite apt to be interrupted by some idiot doing it.   Elbert Green Hubbard

Nature's laws govern which things can be done, and which can't. The trouble is, when we set out to do something, we don't always know which of these categories it's in.   Donald E. Simanek

Nobody knows why, but the only theories which work are the mathematical ones.
                    Michael Holt

Trying to capture the physicists' precise mathematical description of the quantum world with our crude words and mental images is like playing Chopin with a boxing glove on one hand and a catcher's mitt on the other.   George Johnson

There's no system foolproof enough to defeat a sufficiently great fool.
                    Edward Teller

It was absolutely marvelous working for Pauli. You could ask him anything. There was no worry that he would think a particular question was stupid, since he thought all questions were stupid.   Victor Frederick Weisskopf

No amount of experimentation can ever prove me right; a single experiment can prove me wrong.   Albert Einstein

Albert Einstein

The great tragedy of science – the slaying of a beautiful hypothesis by an ugly fact.   Thomas Henry Huxley

If your result needs a statistician then you should design a better experiment.
                                                      Sir Ernest Rutherford

A theory can be proved by experiment; but no path leads from experiment to the birth of a theory.   Manfred Eigen

Manfred Eigen

Whoever undertakes to set himself up as a judge of truth and knowledge is shipwrecked by the laughter of the gods.   Albert Einstein

God help me in my search for truth, and protect me from those who believe they have found it.   Old English Prayer

Most truths are so naked that people feel sorry for them and cover them up, at least a little bit.   Edward R. Murrow

Religions die when they are proved to be true. Science is the record of dead religions.   Oscar Wilde

There are no creeds in physics.   Anonymous

For truth is always strange; stranger than fiction.   Lord Byron

Lord Byron

When one studies strongly radioactive substances special precautions must be taken. Dust, the air of the room, and one's clothes, all become radioactive.
                                                                        Marie Curie

Marie Curie is, of all celebrated beings, the only one whom fame has not corrupted.   Albert Einstein

There are many different kinds of radioactive waste and each has its own half-life so, just to be on the safe side and to simplify matters, I base my calculations on the worst one and that's plutonium.   David R. Brower

On black holes: Evidently, God not only plays dice but plays blind-folded, and, at times, throws them where you can't see them.   Stephen W. Hawking

Black holes are where God divided by zero.   Steven Wright

Experience by itself is not science.   Edmund Husserl

Natural objects, for example, must be experienced before any theorising about them can occur.   Edmund Husserl

Edmund Husserl

What I tell you three times is true.   Lewis Carroll

Lewis Carroll

A hypothesis or theory is clear, decisive, and positive, but it is believed by no one but the man who created it. Experimental findings, on the other hand, are messy, inexact things, which are believed by everyone except the man who did that work.

Harlow Shapley

Sometimes I've believed as many as six impossible things before breakfast.

Lewis Carroll

The situation is not weirder than you imagine, it is weirder than you can imagine.

Lewis Carroll Epstein

Nothing is too wonderful to be true if it be consistent with the laws of nature.

Michael Faraday

Omnibus ex nihil decendis sufficit unum. (It is sufficient to have one thing, to be able to derive everything from nothing.)   Gottfried Wilhelm Leibniz

The important thing is not to stop questioning.   Albert Einstein

Why, Sir, there is every possibility that you will soon be able to tax it! [to PM William Gladstone, on the usefulness of electricity].   Michael Faraday

Michael Faraday

The good Christian should be aware of mathematicians and all those who make empty promises. The danger already exists that the mathematicians have made a covenant with the devil to darken the spirit and to confine man in the bonds of hell.   St. Augustine

Nuclear physics is interesting but it is unlikely to help society. John Cameron

It is likely that we need more radiation to improve our longevity.

John Cameron

No biodiversity without radioactivity. Claus Grupen

Radioactivity drives evolution. Claus Grupen

Claus Grupen

Radiation is a hazard, but as with most hazards it can be measured, analysed and controlled. About a nuclear reprocessing plant

Ketchup left overnight on dinner plates has a longer half-life than radioactive waste. Wes Smith

Mathematics may be defined as the subject in which we never know what we are talking about, nor whether what we are saying is true. Bertrand A. W. Russell

The only reason for time is so that everything doesn't happen at once.
Albert Einstein

Time is nature's way of making certain that everything doesn't happen all at once.
Woody Allen

If I have a thousand ideas and only one turns out to be good, I am satisfied.
Alfred Nobel

The physicist's greatest tool is his wastebasket. Albert Einstein

No progress without mutation. Claus Grupen

Nature uses as little as possible of anything.   Johannes Kepler

Research! A mere excuse for idleness; it has never achieved, and will never achieve any results of the slightest value.   Benjamin Jowett

That is how the atom is split. But what does it mean? To us who think in terms of practical use it means – nothing!   Ritchie Calder

Man is slightly nearer to the atom than the stars. From his central position he can survey the grandest works of Nature with the astronomer, or the minutest works with the physicist.   Sir Arthur Eddington

God has organised the world according to measure, weight and number.

                                                                    Adam Riese

Adam Riese

Man is the measure of all things.   Protagoras of Abdera

One foot is short; one inch is long.   Qu Yuan

Qu Yuan

In some sense man is a microcosm of the universe; therefore what man is, is a clue to the universe. We are enfolded in the universe.   David Bohm

They say that something as small as a butterfly beating its wings in China can cause a hurricane in America, so maybe we should go to China and kill all the butterflies, just to be safe.   Ken Advent

If we knew what it was we were doing, it would not be called research, would it?   Albert Einstein

The rewarding research is that, which by pleasing the thinker, is also of benefit to mankind.   Christian Doppler

Christian Doppler

Science has 'explained' nothing; the more we know the more fantastic the world becomes and the profounder the surrounding darkness.   Aldous Huxley

Now it is established in the sciences that no knowledge is acquired save through the study of its causes and beginnings, if it has had causes and beginnings; nor completed except by knowledge of its accidents and accompanying essentials.
                                                                        Avicenna

The existence of inherent limits of experience in no way settles the question about the subordination of facts of the human world to our knowledge of matter.
                                                                        Wilhelm Dilthey

If the facts don't fit the theory, change the facts.   Albert Einstein

Facts speak louder than statistics.   Geoffrey Streatfield

No observations are absolutely trustworthy.   Francis John Anscombe

Prediction is difficult, especially the future.   Niels Bohr
                              (also attributed to Werner Heisenberg)

Niels Bohr

The physicist does not have the habit of giving up something unless he gets something better in return.   John Archibald Wheeler

There is inherent in nature a hidden harmony that reflects itself in our minds under the image of simple mathematical laws. That then is the reason why events in nature are predictable by a combination of observation and mathematical analysis. Again and again in the history of physics this conviction, or should I say this dream, of harmony in nature has found fulfillments beyond our expectations.
                                                    Hermann Weyl

The simplicities of natural laws arise through the complexities of the language we use for their expression.   Eugene Paul Wigner

Atoms are not things.   Werner Heisenberg

The hope that new experiments will lead us back to objective events in time and space is about as well founded as the hope of discovering the end of the world in the unexplored regions of the Antarctic.   Werner Heisenberg

Who cares about half a second after the Big Bang; what about the half second before?   Fay Weldon

A science is any discipline in which the fool of this generation can go beyond the point reached by the genius of the last generation.   Max Gluckman

If I have seen further it is by standing on the shoulders of giants.

Sir Isaac Newton

Sir Isaac Newton

In science one knows that progress rests on the shoulders of others ...

Arnold Zweig

Arnold Zweig

Our job in physics is to see things simply, to understand a great many complicated phenomena, in terms of a few simple principles.   Steven Weinberg

Science may be described as the art of systematic over-simplification.

Sir Karl Popper

I cannot believe God is a weak left-hander.   Wolfgang Pauli

'God' may be thought of as the cosmic watchmaker, the engineer who constructed the initial state and lit the fuse.   Carl Sagan

Carl Sagan

As physics advances farther and farther every day and develops new axioms, it will require fresh assistance from mathematics.   Francis Bacon

Francis Bacon

From now on there will be no physical treatise which is not primarily mathematical. [after the formulation of the quantum theory]   Paul Adrien Maurice Dirac

There is nothing new to be discovered in physics now. All that remains is more and more precise measurement.   Lord Kelvin

The steady progress of physics requires for its theoretical formulations a mathematics that gets continuously more advanced.   Paul Adrien Maurice Dirac

This century has been so rich in discovery and so packed with technical innovation that it is tempting to believe that there can never be another like it. That conceit betrays the poverty of our collective imagination. The record of previous centuries suggests that the excitement in the years ahead will spring from the answers to the questions we do not yet know enough to ask. John Maddox

John Maddox

Rules and models destroy genius and art. William Hazlitt

All models are wrong, but some are useful. George E. P. Box

A theory has only the alternative of being right or wrong. A model has a third possibility: it may be right, but irrelevant. Manfred Eigen

This isn't right. This isn't even wrong. Wolfgang Pauli

Wolfgang Pauli

For every complex problem, there is a solution that is simple, neat, and wrong.

Henry Louis Mencken

It is often stated that of all the theories proposed in this century, the silliest is quantum theory. In fact, some say that the only thing that quantum theory has going for it is that it is unquestionably correct.   Michio Kaku

Wave mechanics was the most astonishing among all the astonishing discoveries of the twentieth century.   Arnold Sommerfeld

Arnold Sommerfeld

God runs electromagnetics by wave theory on Monday, Wednesday, and Friday, and the Devil runs them by quantum theory on Tuesday, Thursday, and Saturday.

Sir William Bragg

Quantum mechanics and relativity, taken together, are extraordinarily restrictive, and they therefore provide us with a great logical machine. We can explore with our minds any number of possible universes consisting of all kinds of mythical particles and interactions, but all except a very few can be rejected on a priori grounds because they are not simultaneously consistent with special relativity and quantum mechanics. Hopefully in the end we will find that only one theory is consistent with both and that theory will determine the nature of our particular universe.   Steven Weinberg

If the basic idea of a theory is too complicated to fit on a T-shirt it's probably wrong.   Leon Lederman

I don't know how the third world war will be fought, but I do know that the fourth one will be fought with sticks and stones ...   Albert Einstein

It is a bad theory that admits no improvement. Claus Grupen

All good ideas arrive by chance. Max Ernst

Max Ernst

Unless your ideas are ridiculed by the experts they are worth nothing.
Reg Revans

If at first the idea is not absurd, then there is no hope for it. Albert Einstein

Serious people have few ideas. People with ideas are never serious.
Paul Valéry

Paul Valéry

Make it a practice to keep on the lookout for novel and interesting ideas that others
have used successfully. Your idea has to be original only in its adaptation to the
problem you are working on. Thomas Alva Edison

Science is really in the business of disproving its current models or changing them to conform to new information. In essence, we are constantly proving our latest ideas wrong.   David Suzuki

The major difference between a thing that might go wrong and a thing that cannot possibly go wrong is that when a thing that cannot possibly go wrong goes wrong it usually turns out to be impossible to get at or repair.   Douglas Adams

I wish there were a knob on the TV to turn up intelligence. There's a knob called 'brightness', but it doesn't work.   Noel Gallagher

Anyone who expects a source of power from the transformation of the atom is talking moonshine.   Sir Ernest Rutherford

I do not think that the wireless waves I have discovered will have any practical application.   Heinrich Rudolf Hertz

The wireless telegraph is not difficult to understand. The ordinary telegraph is like a very long cat. You pull the tail in New York, and it meows in Los Angeles. The wireless is the same, only without the cat.   Albert Einstein

The belief in a certain idea gives to the researcher the support for his work. Without this belief he would be lost in a sea of doubts and insufficiently verified proofs.
                                                                                          Konrad Zuse

I believe scientists have a duty to share the excitement and pleasure of their work with the general public, and I enjoy the challenge of presenting difficult ideas in an understandable way.   Antony Hewish

Antony Hewish

A thesis has to be presentable … but don't attach too much importance to it. If you do succeed in the sciences, you will do later on better things and then it will be of little moment. If you don't succeed in the sciences, it doesn't matter at all.

Paul Ehrenfest

Paul Ehrenfest

I don't mind your thinking slowly; I mind your publishing faster than you think.

Wolfgang Pauli

OK, so you're a Ph.D. Just don't touch anything.   Anonymous

Each success buys only an admission ticket to a more difficult problem.

Henry Kissinger

Henry Kissinger

If A equals success, then the formula is A = X + Y + Z. X is work. Y is play. Z is keep your mouth shut.   Albert Einstein

Fourth Law of Thermodynamics: If the probability of success is not almost one, it is damn near zero.   David Ellis

Civilisation is just a temporary failure of entropy.   Christine Nelson

Christine Nelson

If your theory is found to be against the second law of thermodynamics, I give you no hope; there is nothing for it but to collapse in deepest humiliation.
                                                                Sir Arthur Eddington

Thermodynamics is a funny subject. The first time you go through it, you don't understand it at all. The second time you go through it, you think you understand it, except for one or two small points. The third time you go through it, you know you don't understand it, but by that time you are so used to it, it doesn't bother you any more.   Arnold Sommerfeld

Nature doesn't exist. It happens.   Herman Weyl

Whatever nature has in store for mankind, unpleasant as it may be, man must accept, for ignorance is never better than knowledge.   Enrico Fermi

There comes a time when the mind takes a higher plane of knowledge but can never prove how it got there. All great discoveries have involved such a leap. The important thing is not to stop questioning.   Albert Einstein

There are grounds for cautious optimism that we may now be near the end of the search for the ultimate laws of nature.   Stephen W. Hawking

It is a profound and necessary truth that the deep things in science are not found because they are useful; they are found because it was possible to find them.

                                                                Robert Oppenheimer

Nature likes to hide itself.   Heraclitus of Ephesus

Physics does not explain the secrets of nature, it leads to more fundamental underlying secrets.   Carl Friedrich von Weizsäcker

Carl Friedrich von Weizsäcker

Physics does not change the nature of the world it studies, and no science of behaviour can change the essential nature of man, even though both sciences yield technologies with a vast power to manipulate the subject matters.

                                                                        Pope Paul VI

Hähnchen [German diminutive for Hahn], let me do it. You don't understand physics. [To Otto Hahn; Otto Hahn was a chemist.]   Lise Meitner

Otto Hahn

Hahn has a special nose for discovering new elements.   Sir Ernest Rutherford

I do not foresee meson guns or hyperon boilers, but if applications for these particles are ever found, it is unlikely that even the most imaginative of present science-
fiction writers will have envisaged them correctly.   Otto Frisch

The electroweak theory states that the Higgs is a matter particle, but in many
respects the Higgs particle behaves more like a new kind of field rather than like
a particle.   Claus Grupen

It would appear that we have reached the limits of what it is possible to achieve
with computer technology, although one should be careful with such statements,
as they tend to sound pretty silly in 5 years. [In 1949]   John von Neumann

The question of whether computers can think is just like the question whether
submarines can swim.   Edsger Dijkstra

Edsger Dijkstra

I do not fear computers. I fear the lack of them.   Isaac Asimov

We may hope that machines will eventually compete with men in all purely intellectual fields. But which are the best ones to start with? Many people think that a
very abstract activity, like the playing of chess, would be best. It can also be maintained that it is best to provide the machine with the best sense organs that money
can buy, and then teach it to understand and speak English.   Alan M. Turing

Computer science is no more about computers than astronomy is about telescopes.
                                                                  Edsger Dijkstra

A table of random numbers, once printed, requires no errata.   Mark Kak

Anyone who attempts to generate random numbers by deterministic means is, of
course, living in a state of sin.   John von Neumann

John von Neumann

There are 10^{11} stars in the galaxy. That used to be a huge number. But it's
only a hundred billion. It's less than the national deficit! We used to call them
astronomical numbers. Now we should call them economical numbers.

Richard P. Feynman

With every passing hour our solar system comes forty-three thousand miles closer
to globular cluster M13 in the constellation Hercules, and still there are some
misfits who continue to insist that there is no such thing as progress.

Ransom K. Ferm

How many pairs of rabbits can be bred from one pair in a year? A man has one
pair of rabbits at a certain place entirely surrounded by a wall. We wish to know
how many pairs will be bred from it in one year, if the nature of these rabbits is
such that they breed every month one other pair and begin to breed in the second
month after their birth.   Leonardo di Pisa, also called Fibonacci

Leonardo di Pisa, also called Fibonacci

Heavier-than-air flying machines are impossible.   Lord Kelvin

The most important fundamental laws and facts of physical science have all been discovered, and these are now so firmly established that the possibility of their ever being supplemented in consequence of new discoveries is exceedingly remote. [In 1903]   Albert Abraham Michelson

The function of an expert is not to be more right than other people, but to be wrong for more sophisticated reasons.   David Butler

There are many examples of old, incorrect theories that stubbornly persisted, sustained only by the prestige of foolish but well-connected scientists. ... Many of these theories have been killed off only when some decisive experiment exposed their incorrectness. ... Thus the yeoman work in any science, and especially physics, is done by the experimentalist, who must keep the theoreticians honest.
                                    Michio Kaku

Theories are never abandoned until their proponents are all dead. Science advances "funeral by funeral".   Max Born

Three things cannot be long hidden: the Sun, the Moon, and the truth.
                                    Buddha

Buddha

I believe that a scientist looking at nonscientific problems is just as dumb as the next guy.   Richard P. Feynman

When I examine myself and my methods of thought, I come to the conclusion that the gift of phantasy has meant more to me than my talent for absorbing positive knowledge.   Albert Einstein

Basic research is what I'm doing when I don't know what I'm doing.

Wernher von Braun

I am enough of an artist to draw freely upon my imagination. Imagination is more important than knowledge. Knowledge is limited. Imagination encircles the world.   Albert Einstein

Discovery consists of seeing what everybody has seen and thinking what nobody has thought.   Albert Szent-Györgyi

What is time? If nobody is asking me, I do know. If I try to explain someone else who is asking me, I do not know.   St. Augustine

St. Augustine

When a work appears to be ahead of its time, it is only the time that is behind the work.   Jean Cocteau

Jean Cocteau

All of modern physics is governed by that magnificent and thoroughly confusing discipline called quantum mechanics … It has survived all tests and there is no reason to believe that there is any flaw in it. … We all know how to use it and how to apply it to problems; and so we have learned to live with the fact that nobody can understand it.   Murray Gell-Mann

Those who are not shocked by quantum theory do not understand it.
                                                        Niels Bohr

Cosmology, nuclear physics, I do try to keep up on. They get more complex, and then some of the old theories just don't work out.   Frederik Pohl

It is the fact that the electrons cannot all get on top of each other that makes tables and everything else solid.   Richard P. Feynman

Several billion trillion tons of superhot exploding hydrogen nuclei rose slowly above the horizon and managed to look small, cold, and slightly damp.
                                                        Douglas Adams

God gives the nuts, but he does not crack them.   Franz Kafka

Franz Kafka

Many inventions had their birth as a toy.   Eric Heffer

The opposite of a correct statement is a false statement. The opposite of a profound truth may well be another profound truth.   Niels Bohr

There's no sense in being precise when you don't even know what you're talking about.   John von Neumann

At last I perceive that in revolutions the supreme power rests with the most abandoned.
Georges Jacques Danton

Georges Jacques Danton

Not everything that can be counted counts, and not everything that counts can be counted.
Albert Einstein

Facts themselves are meaningless. It's only the interpretation we give those facts which counts.
Erle Stanley Gardner

If it can't be expressed in figures, it is not science, it is opinion.   Lazarus Long

Few are those who can see with their own eyes and hear with their own hearts.
Albert Einstein

If you don't know where you are going, any road will get you there.
Lewis Carroll

It is certain, that nothing is certain, not even this statement.
Joachim Ringelnatz

Joachim Ringelnatz

Are the four dimensions that we are used to just the Platonic shadows of a higher-dimensional world?   Claus Grupen

The mathematician has reached the highest rung on the ladder of human thought.
                                                                Havelock Ellis

God exists since mathematics is consistent, and the Devil exists since we cannot prove it.   André Weil (commenting on Kurt Gödel's work)

Examples ... which might be multiplied ad libitum, show how difficult it often is for an experimenter to interpret his results without the aid of mathematics.
                                                                Lord Rayleigh

Lord Rayleigh

Mathematics deals exclusively with the relations of concepts to each other without consideration of their relation to experience.   Albert Einstein

Mathematicians are like Frenchmen: whatever you say to them they translate into their own language and forthwith it is something entirely different.
                                                    Johann Wolfgang von Goethe

Johann Wolfgang von Goethe

Young man, in mathematics you don't understand things, you just get used to them.   John von Neumann

Math is like love – a simple idea but it can get complicated.   Robert J. Drábek

The mathematical sciences particularly exhibit order, symmetry, and limitation; and these are the greatest forms of the beautiful.   Aristotle

Cosmic religiousness is the strongest and most noble driving force of scientific research.   Albert Einstein

The world is my country, science is my religion.   Christiaan Huygens

Christiaan Huygens

The most important scientific revolutions all include, as their only common feature, the dethronement of human arrogance from one pedestal after another of previous convictions about our centrality in the cosmos.   Stephen Jay Gould

An anagram for astronomer: Moonstarer!   Anonymous

The long haired star.   The Anglo-Saxon Chronicle describes Halley's Comet

To be conscious that you are ignorant is a great step to knowledge.
                                                              Benjamin Disraeli

In long intervals I have expressed an opinion on public issues whenever they appeared to be so bad and unfortunate that silence would have made me feel guilty of complicity.   Albert Einstein

If there are any gods whose chief concern is man, they cannot be very important
gods.   Arthur C. Clarke

The universe consists only of atoms and the void; all else is opinion and illusion.
                                                                Edward Robert Harrison

So, this doesn't mean anything, but at least it's not obvious nonsense.
                                                                          Anonymous

The answers are always inside the problem, not outside.   Marshall McLuhan

Einstein was a man who could ask immensely simple questions. And what his
work showed us is that when the answers were simple too, then you can hear God
thinking.   Jacob Bronowski

God is subtle, but He is not malicious.   Albert Einstein

God made the integers; all else is the work of Man.   Leopold Kronecker

But, in terms of information theory, this is precisely where the problem lay: How
were we to reconstruct reality from incomplete or false reports?   Konrad Zuse

Konrad Zuse

Reality is merely an illusion, albeit a very persistent one.   Albert Einstein

The difference between fiction and reality? Fiction has to make sense.
                                                                          Tom Clancy

When I die I'm going to leave my body to science fiction.   Steven Wright

Isn't it interesting that the same people who laugh at science fiction listen to weather forecasts and economists? Kelvin Throop III

Truth is so hard to tell, it sometimes needs fiction to make it plausible. Francis Bacon

Philosophers say a great deal about what is absolutely necessary for science, and it is always, so far as one can see, rather naive, and probably wrong. Richard P. Feynman

You should never bet against anything in science at odds of more than about 10^{12} to 1. Sir Ernest Rutherford

Phantasy is more important than knowledge, because knowledge is limited. Albert Einstein

Heisenberg might have been here. Jay Leno

Any small object that is accidentally dropped will hide under a larger object. Milt Barber

The larger the searchlight, the larger the circumference of the unknown. Dick Taylor

As the circle of my knowledge grows, so grows the circumference of the unknown. Sir Isaac Newton

Everything you imagine is real. Pablo Picasso

Pablo Picasso

Sociology is the science with the greatest number of methods and the least results.
Jules Henri Poincaré

Behavioral psychology is the science of pulling habits out of rats.
Douglas Busch

The only thing you will ever be able to say in the so-called 'social' science is 'some do, some don't'.
Sir Ernest Rutherford

Sir Ernest Rutherford

All hope abandon, ye who enter here!
Dante Alighieri

Dante Alighieri

All theoretical chemistry is really physics; and all theoretical chemists know it.
Richard P. Feynman

Enzymes are things invented by biologists that explain things which otherwise require harder thinking.   Jerome Lettvin

Dare to be naive.   Richard Buckminster Fuller

Amazing Electronic Fact: If you scuffed your feet long enough without touching anything, you would build up so many electrons that your finger would explode! But this is nothing to worry about unless you have carpeting.
Dave Barry [What is Electricity?]

If I had only known, I would have been a locksmith.   Albert Einstein

We can lick gravity, but sometimes the paperwork is overwhelming.
Wernher von Braun

It is impossible to travel faster than light, and certainly not desirable, as one's hat keeps blowing off.   Woody Allen

Nothing travels faster than the speed of light with the possible exception of bad news, which obeys its own special laws.   Douglas Adams

So far as I can remember, there is not one word in the Gospels in praise of intelligence.   Bertrand A. W. Russell

The world holds two classes of men – intelligent men without religion, and religious men without intelligence.   Abu Al-Ala Ahmed Al-Ma'arri

The world is divided into men who have wit and no religion and men who have religion and no wit.   Avicenna

Avicenna

The more we disagree, the more chance there is that at least one of us is right.

Anonymous

Scientific knowledge is a kind of discourse.   Jean-François Lyotard

What is required of a working hypothesis is a fine capacity for discrimination.

Jean-François Lyotard

Jean-François Lyotard

The Earth which sustains humanity must not be injured, it must not be destroyed.

Hildegard of Bingen

Hildegard of Bingen

Delay is preferable to error.   Thomas Jefferson

The distance between insanity and genius is measured only by success.

Bruce Feirstein

Personally, I don't think there's intelligent life on other planets. Why should other planets be any different from this one?   Bob Monkhouse

The world is disgracefully managed; one hardly knows to whom to complain.

Ronald Firbank

If you shut the door to all errors, truth will be shut out. Rabindranath Tagore

Rabindranath Tagore

Small opportunities are often the beginning of great enterprises.

Demosthenes

Opportunities multiply as they are seized. Sun Tzu

Four things do not come back – the spoken word, the sped arrow, the past life, and the neglected opportunity. Abul Wafa Muhammad Al-Buzjani

Abul Wafa Muhammad Al-Buzjani

If you really want something, and really work hard, and take advantage of opportunities, and never give up, you will find a way.   Jane Goodall

Jane Goodall

Chapter 3

Philosophy Quotes

3.1 Body

Science can analyse the alternatives of sound and silence that go to make up a piece of music, but it is quite powerless to explain why one piece is an immortal masterpiece and another in similar form is ephemeral rubbish. Science can analyse chemical components of a human being, but give no qualitative account of his personality. Leonard Alfred George Strong

Heredity is nothing but stored environment. Luther Burbank

Nowadays the rage for possession has got to such a pitch that there is nothing in the realm of nature, whether sacred or profane, out of which profit cannot be squeezed. Erasmus of Rotterdam

Money brings some happiness but after a certain point it just brings more money. Neil Simon

When the missionaries came to Africa they had the Bible and we had the land. They said, 'Let us pray.' We closed our eyes. When we opened them we had the Bible and they had the land. Bishop Desmond Tutu

Bishop Desmond Tutu

119

I was warmed by the sun, rocked by the winds and sheltered by the trees as other
Indian babes. I was living peaceably when people began to speak bad of me. Now
I can eat well, sleep well and be glad. I can go everywhere with a good feeling.

Geronimo the Apache

Geronimo the Apache

We laugh at the Indian philosopher, who to account for the support of the earth,
contrived the hypothesis of a huge elephant, and to support the elephant, a huge
tortoise. If we will candidly confess the truth, we know as little of the operation
of the nerves, as he did of the manner in which the earth is supported: and our
hypothesis about animal spirits, or about the tension and vibrations of the nerves,
are as like to be true, as his about the support of the earth. His elephant was a
hypothesis, and our hypotheses are elephants. Every theory in philosophy, which
is built on pure conjecture, is an elephant; and every theory that is supported partly
by fact, and partly by conjecture, is like Nebuchadnezzar's image, whose feet were
partly of iron, and partly of clay.   Thomas Reid

The natural philosophers are mostly gone. We modern scientists are adding too
many decimals.   Martin H. Fischer

In many aspects, the theoretical physicist is merely a philosopher in a working suit.   Peter Bergmann

Philosophy is nothing but common sense in a dress suit.   Oliver S. Braston

Empty is the argument of the philosopher which does not relieve any human suffering.   Epicurus

He who enters his wife's dressing room is a philosopher or a fool.
                                                            Honoré de Balzac

Woman rule the world. No man has ever done anything that a woman either hasn't allowed him to do, or encouraged him to do.   Bob Dylan

Bob Dylan

Wives are young men's mistresses, companions for middle age, and old men's nurses.   Francis Bacon

I can confirm that Emmy Noether is a great mathematician, however, I cannot confirm by oath that she is a woman. [supporting Emmy Noether, who wasn't allowed in the senate of the University of Göttingen because of being a woman]
                                                            Edmund Landau

Emmy Noether

We will have true equality when we have as many incompetent women in positions of power as we have incompetent men.   Sheelagh D. Whittaker

Strengthen the female mind by enlarging it, and there will be an end to blind obedience.   Mary Wollstonecraft

Mary Wollstonecraft

Yes, as through this world I've wandered I've seen lots of funny men; Some will rob you with a six-gun, And some with a fountain pen.   Woody Guthrie

Woody Guthrie

A man who has never gone to school may steal from a freight car; but if he has a university education, he may steal the whole railroad.   Theodore Roosevelt

School is a building that has four walls – with tomorrow inside.   Lon Watters

In my early days, I was eager to learn and to do things, and therefore I learned quickly.   Sitting Bull

Real education must ultimately be limited to men who insist on knowing, the rest is mere sheep-herding.   Ezra Pound

It is not knowledge, but the act of learning, not possession but the act of getting there, which grants the greatest enjoyment. When I have clarified and exhausted a subject, then I turn away from it, in order to go into darkness again; the never-satisfied man is so strange if he has completed a structure, then it is not in order to dwell in it peacefully, but in order to begin another. I imagine the world conqueror must feel thus, who, after one kingdom is scarcely conquered, stretches out his arms for others.   Karl Friedrich Gauss

The distance is great from the firm belief to the realisation from concrete experience.   Isabella I of Spain

Isabella I

They teach anything in universities today. You can major in mud pies.

Orson Welles

The hardest job kids face today is learning good manners without seeing any.

Fred Astaire

Furious activity is no substitute for understanding.   Henry Horace Williams

If you want to have clean ideas, change them as often as you change your shirts.

Francis Picabia

Life is like riding a bicycle. To keep your balance you must keep moving.

Albert Einstein

Albert Einstein

Practice, the master of all things.   Augustus Octavius

Augustus

Reading is to the mind what exercise is to the body.   Sir Richard Steele

True enjoyment comes from activity of the mind and exercise of the body; the two are ever united.   Wilhelm von Humboldt

Wilhelm von Humboldt

Whatever you can do, or dream you can do, do it. Boldness has genius, power and magic in it. Begin it now.   Johann Wolfgang von Goethe

The man who moves a mountain begins by carrying away small stones.
                                                                  Anonymous

Do not go where the path may lead; instead go where there is no path and leave a trail.   Ralph Waldo Emerson

No man ever steps in the same river twice, for it's not the same river and he's not the same man.   Heraclitus of Ephesus

In its function, the power to punish is not essentially different from that of curing or educating.   Michel Foucault

Michel Foucault

Most institutions demand unqualified faith; but the institution of science makes skepticism a virtue.   Robert King Merton

I have gained this by philosophy: that I do without being commanded what others do only from fear of the law.   Aristotle

Every (reasonable) man is his own law court and punishes himself enough.
                                                                      Patricia Highsmith

The more corrupt the state, the more numerous the laws.   Tacitus

The great questions of the day will not be settled by means of speeches and majority decisions but by iron and blood.   Fürst Otto von Bismarck

Fürst Otto von Bismarck

An eye for an eye makes the whole world blind.   Mahatma Gandhi

The need to be right is the sign of a vulgar mind.   Albert Camus

If you ain't wrong, you're right.   Sunny Skylar

Ways and means cannot be found
With such chaos all around.
There's treason and deceit,
There's violence on the street.
Peace and justice are deplored;
The three will never be achieved until these two have been restored.

Walther von der Vogelweide

Walther von der Vogelweide

All power is limited by definite boundaries and laws. No power is absolute, infinite, unbridled, arbitrary, and lawless. Every power is bound to laws, right, and equity.   Johannes Althusius

Johannes Althusius

Every law is an infraction of liberty.   Jeremy Bentham

Jeremy Bentham

The longer we dwell on our misfortunes, the greater the power to harm us.

Voltaire

The almost insoluble task is to let neither the power of others, nor our own powerlessness, stupefy us.   Theodor W. Adorno

A person may cause evil to others not only by his actions but by his inaction, and in either case he is justly accountable to them for the injury.   John Stuart Mill

A multitude of rulers is not a good thing. Let there be one ruler, one king.

Homer

Homer

He who fights with monsters should look to it that he himself does not become a monster.   Friedrich Nietzsche

Maybe this world is just another planet's hell.   Aldous Huxley

The nature of bad news infects the teller.   Cleopatra

Cleopatra

Disobedience is the true foundation of liberty. The obedient must be slaves.
                                                          Henry David Thoreau

The art of being a slave is to rule one's master.   Diogenes

Diogenes

Those who do not move, do not notice their chains.   Rosa Luxemburg

Man is condemned to be free; because once thrown into the world, he is responsible for everything he does.   Jean-Paul Sartre

You should never wear your best trousers when you go out to fight for freedom and liberty.   Henrik Ibsen

Tyranny and anarchy are never far apart.   Jeremy Bentham

Liberty for wolves is death to the lambs.   Isaiah Berlin

Isaiah Berlin

You have power over people only as long as you don't take everything away from them. But when you have robbed a man of everything he's no longer in your power – he's free again.   Alexander Solzhenitsyn

A man can be destroyed but not defeated.   Ernest Hemingway

Ernest Hemingway

You can kill the body but not the spirit.   Robert Louis Stevenson

Sometimes the truth hurts. And sometimes it feels real good.   Henry Rollins

My writing is an answer to the partisans of the many, with a view to showing that the hypothesis of the many, if examined in sufficient detail, leads to even more absurd results than the hypothesis of the one.   Zeno of Elea

Zeno of Elea

The hour of departure has arrived, and we go our ways – I to die, and you to live. Which is better God only knows.   Socrates

Socrates

If the highest aim of a captain were to preserve his ship, he would keep it in port forever.   St. Thomas Aquinas

We only think when we are confronted with problems.   John Dewey

At each increase of knowledge, as well as on the contrivance of every new tool, human labour becomes abridged.   Charles Babbage

Never stand begging for that which you have the power to earn.
                                                      Miguel de Cervantes Saavedra

If people never did silly things nothing intelligent would ever get done.

Ludwig Wittgenstein

We are creating the future.

Günter Grass

Günter Grass

The greatest danger to our future is apathy.   Jane Goodall

Although God demands a whole heart, He will accept a broken one if He gets all the pieces.   Mary Irving

I tremble for my country when I reflect that God is just.   Thomas Jefferson

You shall have joy or you shall have power, said God; you shall not have both.

Ralph Waldo Emerson

I sometimes think that God, in creating man, somewhat overestimated his ability.

Oscar Wilde

Disappointed by apes, God created man. He then forewent further experiments.

Mark Twain

I am a great and sublime fool. But then I am God's fool, and all His work must be contemplated with respect.   Mark Twain

Work banishes three great evils: boredom, vice and poverty.   Voltaire

If work were so good, the rich would have hogged it for themselves years ago.

Marc Twain

A lot of what passes for depression these days is nothing more than a body saying that it needs work.   Geoffrey Norman

Home is where I work and I work everywhere.   Alfred Nobel

If two men on the same job agree all the time, then one is useless. If they disagree all the time, then both are useless.   Darryl Zamuck

Teamwork is an euphemism for the fact that the others actually do the work.
                                                    Norbert Bolz

Norbert Bolz

There can be hardly anything more alien or even more destructive to workmanship than teamwork.   Hannah Arendt

Well done is better than well said.   Benjamin Franklin

Benjamin Franklin

Don't find a fault – find a remedy.   Henry Ford

If everybody contemplates the infinite instead of fixing the drains, many of us will
die of cholera.   John Rich

When it comes to getting things done, we need fewer architects and more brick-
layers.   Colleen Barrett

One never notices what has been done; one can see only what remains to be done.
                                                                  Marie Curie

Marie Curie

Especially now when views are becoming more polarized, we must work to understand each other across political, religious and national boundaries.
                                                                  Jane Goodall

It is not the strongest of the species that survives, nor the most intelligent that
survives. It is the one that is the most adaptable to change.   Charles Darwin

Charles Darwin

Alone the fact that we exist, allows us to be members of the most exclusive of all clubs: those of the survivors.   Hoimar von Ditfurth

If we don't change, we will become extinct like dinosaurs.   Leonardo Boff

Leonardo Boff

There is a simple grandeur in the view of life with its powers of growth, assimilation and reproduction, being originally breathed into matter under one or few forms, and that whilst this our planet has gone circling according to fixed laws, and land and water, in a cycle of change, have gone on replacing each other, that from so simple an origin, through the power of gradual selection of influential changes, endless forms most beautiful and most wonderful have been evolved.

Charles Darwin

Life is a series of natural and spontaneous changes. Don't resist them – that only creates sorrow. Let reality be reality. Let things flow naturally forward in whatever way they like.   Lao-Tzu

Lao-Tzu

The mystery of the beginning of all things is insoluble by us; and I for one must be content to remain an agnostic.   Charles Darwin

By 1871, twelve years after the *Origin of Species*, Darwin no longer needed to convince people of good will and mental flexibility that evolution had occurred; that battle had been won.   Stephen Jay Gould

Judgement comes from experience, and experience comes from bad judgement.
                                                                 Simon Bolivar

Simon Bolivar

To enjoy the world without judgement is what a realised life is like.

                                                                 Joko Beck

You must give some time to your fellow men. Even if it's a little thing, do something for others – something for which you get no pay but the privilege of doing it.   Albert Schweitzer

Albert Schweitzer

There are two kinds of people; those who are always well and those who are always sick. Most of the evils of the world come the first sort and most of the achievements from the second.   Louis Dudek

To be caught between two stools is one of the most honourable places which one can earn nowadays.   Hoimar von Ditfurth

Whoever desires to found a state and give laws must start by assuming that all men are bad and ever ready to display their vicious nature, whenever they may find occasion for it.   Niccolò Machiavelli

Dishonesty is like a boomerang. Just when you think all is well, it hits you on the back of the head.   H. Jackson Brown

There is nothing to it being an honest man, if you have a soup everyday to eat.   Heinrich Böll

The moment is ageless.   Leonardo da Vinci

Don't complain about growing old – many people are denied that privilege.   Earl Warren

The greater the wealth, the thicker will be the dirt.   John Kenneth Galbraith

There will be no veterans of World War Three.   Walter Mondale

Being a hero is the shortest-lived profession on earth.   Will Rogers

A peaceful man is somebody who allows himself to be shot, just to demonstrate that the killer is an aggressor.   Ludwig Marcuse

Ludwig Marcuse

It is my contention that killing under the cloak of war is nothing but an act of murder.
                                                        Albert Einstein

Non-violence is a flop. The only bigger flop is violence.   Joan Baez

No nation has ever prospered in which family life was not held sacred.
                                                        William Ralph Inge

Military intelligence is a contradiction in terms.   Groucho Marx

Groucho Marx

Military justice is to justice what military music is to music.   Groucho Marx

For my part, I wish all guns with their belongings and everything could be sent to hell, which is the proper place for their exhibition and use.   Alfred Nobel

Tough times don't last, tough people do.   Robert Schuller

The child was diseased at birth-stricken with an hereditary ill that only the most vital men are able to shake off. I mean poverty – the most deadly and prevalent of all diseases.   Eugene O'Neill

The most anxious man in the prison is the governor.   George Bernard Shaw

A man should live with his superiors as he does with his fire; not too near, lest he burn; not too far off, lest he freeze.   Diogenes

If you have only a hammer, you tend to see every problem as a nail.
                                                        Abraham Maslow

A serious and good philosophical work could be written consisting entirely of jokes.   Ludwig Wittgenstein

A belly laugh increases the ability of your immune system to fight infections.

Elizabeth Taylor

Without the divine drop of oil we call humour the great world machine would soon grind to a standstill.

Hugo Rahner

Happiness, it seems to me, consists of two things: first, in being where you belong, and second – and best – in comfortably going through everyday life, that is, having had a good night's sleep and not being hurt by new shoes.

Theodor Fontane

Theodor Fontane

The real man smiles in trouble, gathers strength from distress, and grows brave by reflection.

Thomas Paine

Thomas Paine

A child enters your home and for the next twenty years makes so much noise you can hardly stand it. The child departs, leaving the house so silent you think you are going mad.

John Holmes

If you want to succeed, double your failure rate.   Tom Watson

A great city is one that handles art and garbage equally well.   Bob Talbert

A hidden connection is stronger than an obvious one.   Heraclitus of Ephesus

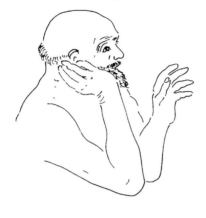

Heraclitus of Ephesus

A man said to the Universe:
"Sir, I exist!"
"However," replied the Universe,
"the fact has not created in me a sense of obligation."   Stephen Crane

If there's a book you want to read but it hasn't been written yet, then you must write it.   Toni Morrison

Don't worry about people stealing your ideas. If your ideas are any good, you'll have to ram them down people's throats.   Howard Aiken

Depressed? Of course we're all depressed. We've been so quickly, violently, and irreconcilably plucked from nature, from physical labor, from kinship and village mentality, from every natural and primordial anti-depressant. The further society "progresses," the grander the scale of imbalance. Just as fluoride is put in water to prevent dental caries, we'll soon find government mandating Prozac in our water to prevent mental caries.   M. Robin D'Antan

The art of medicine consists in amusing the patient while Nature cures the disease.
          Voltaire

To live by medicine is to live horribly.   Carl Linnaeus

Carl Linnaeus

To argue with a person who has renounced the use of reason is like administering medicine to the dead.   Thomas Paine

Medicine is not only a science; it is also an art. It does not consist of compounding pills and plasters; it deals with the very processes of life, which must be understood before they may be guided.   Paracelsus

Paracelsus

The first rule of intelligent tinkering is to save all the parts.   Paul Ehrlich

The dose makes the poison.   Paracelsus

I see harm reduction as a way of engaging people as part of that path to recovery.
Paul Ehrlich

Paul Ehrlich

Medicine rests upon four pillars – philosophy, astronomy, alchemy, and ethics.
Paracelsus

When a physician walks behind the coffin of a patient, sometimes actually the
cause follows the effect.   Robert Koch

Robert Koch

Now I believe I can hear the philosophers protesting that it can only be misery to
live in folly, illusion, deception and ignorance, but it isn't – it's human.
Erasmus of Rotterdam

Philosophers are adults who persist in asking childish questions.   Isaiah Berlin

What difference is there, do you think, between those in Plato's cave who can only marvel at the shadows and images of various objects, provided they are content and don't know what they miss, and the philosopher who has emerged from the cave and sees the real things?   Erasmus of Rotterdam

The seven deadly sins ... Food, clothing, firing, rent, taxes, respectability and children. Nothing can lift those seven millstones from man's neck but money; and the spirit cannot soar until the millstones are lifted.   George Bernard Shaw

3.2   Mind

She was a great man whose only fault was in being a woman. [About Emilie du Châtelét]

Voltaire

If you want them to know you are fancy, don't tell them you're fancy. Tell them a joke.

Ian Davis

Whereof one cannot speak, thereof one must remain silent.

Ludwig Wittgenstein

Order and simplification are the first steps toward the mastery of a subject.

Thomas Mann

Thomas Mann

Some of the world's greatest feats were accomplished by people not smart enough to know they were impossible.   Doug Larson

Our freedom to doubt was born out of a struggle against authority in the early days of science. It was a very deep and strong struggle. It is our responsibility as scientists to proclaim the value of this freedom; to teach how doubt is not to be feared but welcomed and discussed; and to demand this freedom as our duty to all coming generations.   Richard P. Feynman

Authority poisons everybody who takes authority on himself.   Golda Meir

Every exit is an entrance somewhere else.   Tom Stoppard

The outside world is something independent from man, something absolute, and the quest for the laws which apply to this absolute appeared to me as the most sublime scientific pursuit in life.   Max Planck

There are three classes of people. Those who see; those who see when they are shown; and those who do not see.
Leonardo da Vinci

Leonardo da Vinci

We distinguish the excellent man from the common man by saying that the former is the one who makes great demands on himself, and the latter who makes no demands on himself.
José Ortega y Gasset

The philosopher's stone looks very much like the fool's stone.
Joachim Ringelnatz

Thou hast seen nothing yet.
Miguel de Cervantes Saavedra

Miguel de Cervantes Saavedra

In the midnineteenth century, science, theology, philosophy, and social theory had not yet been severed from one another to form autonomous disciplines.
Howard L. Kaye

The most ordinary things are to philosophy a source of insoluble puzzles. With
infinite ingenuity it constructs a concept of space or time and then finds it absolutely impossible that there be objects in this space or that processes occur during
this time ... the source of this kind of logic lies in excessive confidence in the
so-called laws of thought.   Ludwig Boltzmann

Ludwig Boltzmann

To go straight to the deepest depth, I went for Hegel; what unclear thoughtless flow
of words I was to find there! My unlucky star led me from Hegel to Schopenhauer
... Even in Kant there were many things that I could grasp so little that given his
general acuity of mind I almost suspected that he was pulling the reader's leg or
was even an imposter.   Ludwig Boltzmann

Science favours the prepared mind.   Louis Pasteur

It's all to do with the training: you can do a lot if you're properly trained.
                                                            Queen Elizabeth II

Queen Elizabeth II

A mathematician will recognise Cauchy, Gauss, Jacobi or Helmholtz after reading a few pages, just as musicians recognise, from the first few bars, Mozart, Beethoven or Schubert.   Ludwig Boltzmann

Philosophy of science is about as useful to scientists as ornithology is to birds.
                                                                Richard P. Feynman

Philosophy consists very largely of one philosopher arguing that all others are jackasses. He usually proves it, and I should add that he also usually proves that he is one himself.   Henry Louis Mencken

I often say that when you can measure what you are speaking about, and express it in numbers, you know something about it; but when you cannot measure it, when you cannot express it in numbers, your knowledge is of a meagre and unsatisfactory kind.   Lord Kelvin

To understand is to perceive patterns.   Isaiah Berlin

The ability to perceive or think differently is more important than the knowledge gained.   David Bohm

Scientists are explorers. Philosophers are tourists.   Richard P. Feynman

Music is a higher revelation than philosophy.   Ludwig van Beethoven

Ludwig van Beethoven

Capitalism without bankruptcy is like Christianity without hell.
                                                                Frank Borman

An atheist is someone who believes himself an accident.   Francis Thompson

Sometimes one pays most for the things one gets for nothing.   Albert Einstein

Rather than love, than fame, than money, give me truth.

Henry David Thoreau

If we accept that the aim of industrial action, in a given case, is justified, it still matters how it is pursued.   Elizabeth Anscombe

Truth which is merely told is quick to be forgotten; truth which is discovered lasts a lifetime.   William Barclay

There is point in speaking of knowledge only where a contrast exists between 'he knows' and 'he (merely) thinks he knows'.   Elizabeth Anscombe

Elizabeth Anscombe

It is the province of knowledge to speak and it is the privilege of wisdom to listen.

Oliver Wendell Holmes, Jr.

The infallible Holy Fathers of the Middle Ages decreed that it was heresy to print or own a Bible in a modern tongue! Confess your sins and plead for forgiveness – but not before you BURN THAT ABOMINATION! [About Tyndale's English translation of Luther's protestant Bible]

William Warham, Archbishop of Canterbury

It is a test of a good religion whether you can make a joke of it.

Gilbert Keith Chesterton

What embitters the world is not excess of criticism, but an absence of self-criticism.

Gilbert Keith Chesterton

To be a critic is a stupid job if you are just a critic and know nothing else beyond it.   Alfred Kerr

Intelligence hardly guarantees holiness.   John Duns Scotus

John Duns Scotus

The term science should not be given to anything but the aggregate of the recipes that are always successful. All the rest is literature.   Paul Valéry

When a distinguished but elderly scientist states that something is possible, he is almost certainly right. When he states that something is impossible, he is very probably wrong.   Arthur C. Clarke

It is more important to have beauty in one's equations than to have them fit experiment.   Paul Adrien Maurice Dirac

It is possible to know when you are right way ahead of checking all the consequences. You can recognise truth by its beauty and simplicity.
                              Richard P. Feynman

When the war finally came to an end, I was at a loss as to what to do ...   I took stock of my qualifications. A not-very-good degree, redeemed somewhat by my achievements at the Admiralty. A knowledge of certain restricted parts of magnetism and hydrodynamics, neither of them subjects for which I felt the least bit of enthusiasm. No published papers at all ... Only gradually did I realise that this lack of qualification could be an advantage. By the time most scientists have reached age thirty they are trapped by their own expertise. They have invested so much effort in one particular field that it is often extremely difficult, at that time in their careers, to make a radical change. I, on the other hand, knew nothing, except for a basic training in somewhat old-fashioned physics and mathematics and an ability to turn my hand to new things ... Since I essentially knew nothing, I had an almost completely free choice ...   Francis Crick

My work has always tried to unite the true with the beautiful and when I had to choose one or the other, I usually chose the beautiful.   Hermann Weyl

If you are out to describe the truth, leave elegance to the tailor.

Albert Einstein

If your new theorem can be stated with great simplicity, then there will exist a pathological exception.   Adrian Mathesis

My teacher, Hopkins, often commented on the craving for certainty that led so many physicists into mysticism or into the Church and similar organisations ... Faith seems to be an occupational hazard for physicists.

Norman Wingate Pirie

The first key to wisdom is assiduous and frequent questioning ... For by doubting we come to inquiry, and by inquiry we arrive at truth.   Pierre Abélard

Preserve in everything freedom of mind. Never spare a thought for what men may think, but always keep your mind so free inwardly that you could always do the opposite.   St. Ignatius of Loyola

The will is not to be confused with freedom (the power of choice). Freedom can choose only what is possible, while the will can choose also the impossible. The latter is well exemplified in a man who does not will to die. Therefore, the will is more general than freedom, and for this reason all freedom is will, but not all will is freedom.   Abu Nasr Muhammad Al-Farabi

Abu Nasr Muhammad Al-Farabi

The most dangerous tendency of the modern world is the way in which bogus theories are given the force of dogma.   Jean Danielou

What art was to the ancient world, science is to the modern.

Benjamin Disraeli

The art of tomorrow will be a common collective treasure or it will not be art at all.   Victor Vasarely

Victor Vasarely

Art is a marriage of the conscious and the unconscious.   Jean Cocteau

True science teaches, above all, to doubt, and to be ignorant.

Miguel de Unamuno

In science, self-satisfaction is death. Personal self-satisfaction is the death of the scientist. Collective self-satisfaction is the death of the research. It is restlessness, anxiety, dissatisfaction, agony of mind that nourish science.   Jacques Monod

The power to question is the basis of all human progress.   Indira Gandhi

Indira Gandhi

All questions are valid, all answers are tentative.   Hypatia

There are many questions which fools can ask that wise men cannot answer.

George Polyá

Even if we achieve gigantic successes in our work, there is no reason whatsoever to feel conceited and arrogant. Modesty helps one to go forward, whereas conceit makes one lag behind. This is a truth we must always bear in mind.

Mao Tse Tung

It does not matter how slowly you go, so long as you don't stop.   Confucius

Mathematics began to seem too much like puzzle solving. Physics is puzzle solving, too, but of puzzles created by nature, not by the mind of man.

Maria Goeppert-Mayer

Maria Goeppert-Mayer

There are problems to whose solution I would attach an infinitely greater importance than to those of mathematics, for example touching ethics, or our relation to God, or concerning our destiny and our future; but their solution lies wholly beyond us and completely outside the province of science.   Karl Friedrich Gauss

Intellectuals solve problems; geniuses prevent them.   Albert Einstein

Philosophy is nothing but unintelligible answers to insoluble problems.

Henry Brooks Adams

An essential aspect of creativity is not being afraid to fail.   Edwin Land

If I take death into my life, acknowledge it, and face it squarely, I will free myself
from the anxiety of death and the pettiness of life – and only then will I be free to
become myself.   Martin Heidegger

Martin Heidegger

Like many intellectuals, he was incapable of saying a simple thing in a simple
way.   Marcel Proust

It's so simple to be wise. Just think of something stupid to say and then don't say
it.   Sam Levenson

When a philosopher says something that is true then it is trivial. When he says
something that is not trivial then it is false.   Karl Friedrich Gauss

Although most people never overcome the habit of berating the world for their
difficulties, those who are too weak to make a stand against reality have no choice
but to obliterate themselves by identifying with it. They are never rationally rec-
onciled to civilization. Instead, they bow to it, secretly accepting the identity
of reason and domination, of civilization and the ideal, however much they may
shrug their shoulders. Well-informed cynicism is only another mode of confor-
mity.   Max Horkheimer

Max Horkheimer

All the resources we need are in the mind.   Theodore Roosevelt

If you are able, o stranger, to find out all these things and gather them together in your mind, giving all the relations, you shall depart crowned with glory and knowing that you have been perfectly accepted in the realm of wisdom.

Diophantos of Alexandria

Diophantos of Alexandria

The man who does not read good books has no advantage over the man who cannot read them.   Mark Twain

I would rather discover one true cause than gain the kingdom of Persia.

Democritus of Abdera

Democritus of Abdera

I am one of the people who love the why of things.   Catherine the Great

We're one of the most highly regulated industries, and we have to pay attention to what government is doing.   Paul Ehrlich

You cannot adopt politics as a profession and remain honest.   Louis Howe

It is dangerous to be right when the government is wrong.   Voltaire

Every government is run by liars and nothing they say should be believed.

Isador Feinstein (I. F.) Stone

Isador Feinstein (I. F.) Stone

Governments have never learned anything from history, or acted on principles deducted from it.   Georg Wilhelm Friedrich Hegel

He who puts out his hand to stop the wheel of history will have his fingers crushed.

Lech Walesa

Nothing is politically right which is morally wrong.   Daniel O'Connell

The extreme limit of wisdom, that's what the public calls madness.

Jean Cocteau

If civilisation had been left in female hands, we would still be living in grass huts.

Camille Paglia

Camille Paglia

Every civilization that has ever existed has ultimately collapsed.

Henry Kissinger

A marriage without conflicts is almost as inconceivable as a nation without crisis.

André Maurois

Freedom of thought is the only guarantee against an infection of people by mass myths, which, in the hands of treacherous hypocrites and demagogues, can be transformed into bloody dictatorships.   Andrei Sakharov

It is not enough to have knowledge, one must also apply it. It is not enough to have wishes, one must also accomplish.   Johann Wolfgang von Goethe

If you do not expect the unexpected you will not find it, for it is not to be reached by search or trial.   Heraclitus of Ephesus

There is nothing permanent except change.   Heraclitus of Ephesus

Dubito ergo cogito; cogito ergo sum. (I doubt, therefore I think; I think therefore I am).   René Descartes

René Descartes

What was once thought can never be unthought.   Friedrich Dürrenmatt

The married state is the most complete image of heaven and hell we are capable of receiving in this life.   Richard Steele

A free life cannot acquire many possessions, because this is not easy to do without servility to mobs or monarchs.   Epicurus

Victory goes to the player who makes the next-to-last mistake.

Savielly Grigorievitch Tartakower

The risk of a wrong decision is preferable to the terror of indecision.

Maimonides (Moshe Ben Maimon)

The essential fact is simply that all the pictures which science now draws of Nature
... are mathematical pictures ... It can hardly be disputed that Nature and our
conscious mathematical minds work according to the same laws.

Sir James Jeans

Philosophy, that great mother of science.   Francis Bacon

Science is what you know. Philosophy is what you don't know.

Bertrand A. W. Russell

Science is organised knowledge. Wisdom is organised life.   Immanuel Kant

Immanuel Kant

Philosophy is the science which considers truth.   Aristotle

About philosophy Apart from the known and the unknown, what else is there?

Harold Pinter

Almost everyone who didn't know what to do, did philosophy. Well, that's logical.
[On the choice of the subject at university]   Tom Stoppard

The safest general characterisation of the European philosophical tradition is that
it consists of a series of footnotes to Plato.   Alfred North Whitehead

The philosophy of one century is the common sense of the next.

Henry Ward Beecher

The philosophies of one age have become the absurdities of the next, and the
foolishness of yesterday will become the wisdom of tomorrow.

Sir William Osler

At the present moment, the security of coherent philosophy, which existed from Parmenides to Hegel, is lost.   Karl Theodor Jaspers

Only as an individual can man become a philosopher.   Karl Theodor Jaspers

Who questions much, shall learn much, and retain much.   Francis Bacon

To be a philosopher is not merely to have subtle thoughts, nor even to found a school, but to so love wisdom as to live according to its dictates a life of simplicity, independence, magnanimity and trust.   Henry David Thoreau

Education is a better safeguard of liberty than a standing army.

Edward Everett

Education is the attempt, to fight stupidity.   Peter Sloterdijk

Peter Sloterdijk

We have two ears and one tongue so that we would listen more and talk less.

Diogenes

Silence is argument carried out by other means.   Ernesto 'Che' Guevara

Ernesto 'Che' Guevara

Silence is an argument which is hard to beat.   Heinrich Böll

The work of an intellectual is not to mould the political will of others; it is, through the analyses that he does in his own field, to re-examine evidence and assumptions, to shake up habitual ways of working and thinking, to dissipate conventional familiarities, to re-evaluate rules and institutions and to participate in the formation of a political will (where he has his role as citizen to play).   Michel Foucault

For to be free is not merely to cast off one's chains, but to live in a way that respects and enhances the freedom of others.   Nelson Mandela

Nelson Mandela

Freedom is always and exclusively freedom for the one who thinks differently.
                                                                Rosa Luxemburg

Rosa Luxemburg

You can't separate peace from freedom because no one can be at peace unless he has his freedom.   Malcolm X

The rights of democracy are not reserved for a select group within society, they are the rights of all the people.   Olof Palme

For us democracy is a question of human dignity. And human dignity is political freedom.   Olof Palme

Olof Palme

Erasmus was the light of his century; others were its strength: he lighted the way; others knew how to walk on it while he himself remained in the shadow as the source of light always does. But he who points the way into a new era is no less worthy of veneration than he who is the first to enter it; those who work invisibly have also accomplished a feat.   Stefan Zweig

Stefan Zweig

A fool's brain digests philosophy into folly, science into superstition, and art into pedantry. Hence university education.   George Bernard Shaw

A modest confession of ignorance is the ripest and last attainment of philosophy.
                                              Roswell Dwight Hitchcock

Give a man a fish, and you'll feed him for a day. Give him a religion, and he'll starve to death while praying for a fish.   Timothy Jones

This is my simple religion. There is no need for temples; no need for complicated philosophy. Our own brain, our own heart is our temple; the philosophy is kindness.   Dalai Lama

Dalai Lama

People of all religions know far too little about one another; above all, they know far too little about what all religious and ethical traditions have in common.

Hans Küng

No peace among the nations without peace among the religions; No peace among the religions without dialogue between the religions; No dialogue between the religions without global ethical standards; and No survival of our globe without a global ethic.   Hans Küng

Hans Küng

The drop of rain makes a hole in the stone, not by violence, but by falling often.

Hugh Latimer

Hugh Latimer

Never believe anything in politics until it has been officially denied.

Fürst Otto von Bismarck

When you want to fool the world, tell the truth.   Fürst Otto von Bismarck

I think it would be a good idea. [when asked what he thought of Western civilization]   Mahatma Gandhi

The greatest misfortune of all is not to be able to bear misfortune.

Bias of Priene

Wisdom consists of the anticipation of consequences.   Norman Cousins

To comply heroic to the unavoidable is certainly wisdom.   Adolph Kolping

I find television very educating. Every time somebody turns on the set, I go into the other room and read a book.   Groucho Marx

Events in the past may be roughly divided into those which probably never happened and those which do not matter.   William Ralph Inge

Every true man, sir, who is a little above the level of the beasts and plants does not live for the sake of living, without knowing how to live; but he lives so as to give a meaning and a value of his own to life.   Luigi Pirandello

Whereas I know but little of the world below, I do not suppose that I know.

Socrates

If a man's good for nothing else, he can at least teach philosophy.

William James

William James

We are all mediators, translators.   Jacques Derrida

To ridicule philosophy is truly philosophical.   Blaise Pascal

We have to make philosophy itself an object of philosophical concern.

Wilhelm Dilthey

The past is at least secure.   Daniel Webster

It is proof of a base and low mind for one to wish to think with the masses or majority, merely because the majority is the majority. Truth does not change because it is, or is not, believed by a majority of the people.   Giordano Bruno

About Giordano Bruno: He was a philosopher, but annoying to the theologians.

Eugen Drewermann

Brain: an apparatus with which we think we think.   Ambrose Bierce

Men ought to know that from nothing else but the brain come joys, delights, laughter and sports, grief, despondency and lamentations.   Hippocrates

My brain is the key that sets me free.   Houdini

A painter must think of everything he sees as being there entirely for his own use and pleasure.   Frans Hals

Painting is like travelling along a road, which is often rough and full of obstacles, and which can lead you to quite unexpected destinations.   Frans Hals

Frans Hals

Why should I talk about my paintings? They speak for themselves.
Peter Brueghel the Elder

Peter Brueghel the Elder

Every form is a base for colour, every colour is the attribute of a form.
Victor Vasarely

To be good is noble, but to teach others to be good is nobler and less trouble.
Mark Twain

I have come to believe that a great teacher is a great artist and that there are as few as there are any other great artists. Teaching might even be the greatest of the arts since the medium is the human mind and spirit.   John Steinbeck

The Dadaistic view of nature is a consequence of long absorption in images.

Karl Riha

Science knows, poetry feels.

Karl Riha

The worst state of affairs is when science begins to concern itself with art.

Paul Klee

Science is for those who learn; poetry for those who know.   Joseph Roux

The problem with tolerance is that you have to tolerate the intolerant as well.

George M. Weilacher

When I study philosophical works I feel I am swallowing something which I don't have in my mouth.   Albert Einstein

Poetry heals the wounds inflicted by reason.   Novalis

Novalis

As long as a word remains unspoken, you are its master; once you utter it, you are its slave.   Solomon Ibn Gabirol

A jury is composed of twelve men of average ignorance.   Herbert Spencer

Civilization is a progress from an indefinite, incoherent homogeneity toward a definite, coherent heterogeneity.   Herbert Spencer

To be ignorant of one's ignorance is the malady of the ignorant.

Amos Bronson Alcolt

He must be very ignorant for he answers every question he is asked.   Voltaire

Poetry implies the whole truth, philosophy expresses only a particle of it.

Henry David Thoreau

All that we are is the result of what we have thought. The mind is everything. What we think we become.

Buddha

Tell me to what you pay attention and I will tell you who you are.

José Ortega y Gasset

There is little difference between man and beast, but what ambition and glory makes.

Margaret Cavendish

It takes a wise man to recognise a wise man.

Xenophanes

Xenophanes

You know that I write slowly. This is chiefly because I am never satisfied until I have said as much as possible in a few words, and writing briefly takes far more time than writing at length.

Karl Friedrich Gauss

Writing is organized spontaneity.

Martin Walser

We are shaped by our thoughts; we become what we think. When the mind is pure, joy follows like a shadow that never leaves.

Buddha

For example, justice is considered to mean equality. It does mean equality – but equality for those who are equal, and not for all.

Aristotle

If you are neutral in situations of injustice, you have chosen the side of the oppressor. If an elephant has its foot on the tail of a mouse and you say that you are neutral, the mouse will not appreciate your neutrality.

Bishop Desmond Tutu

Peace is not the absence of war; it is a virtue; a state of mind; a disposition for benevolence; confidence; and justice.   Baruch Spinoza

Charity begins at home, and justice begins next door.   Charles Dickens

Conscience is the chamber of justice.   Origen of Alexandria

If you want peace work for justice.   Pope Paul VI

Pope Paul VI

It is both necessary to say and think that being is: for to be is possible, and nothingness is not possible.   Parmenides

Parmenides

Science is the knowledge of consequences, and dependence of one fact upon another.
                                                                Thomas Hobbes

Thomas Hobbes

The ultimate measure of a man is not where he stands in moments of comfort and convenience, but where he stands at times of challenge and controversy.
                                                                Martin Luther King

Martin Luther King

Consider any individual at any period of his life, and you will always find him preoccupied with fresh plans to increase his comfort.   Alexis de Tocqueville

The weakest living creature, by concentrating his powers on a single object, can accomplish good results while the strongest, by dispersing his effort over many chores, may fail to accomplish anything.   Og Mandino

Prejudice is the child of ignorance.   William Hazlitt

I disapprove of what you say, but I will defend to the death your right to say it.
                                                                Evelyn Beatrice Hall

Considering how dangerous everything is, nothing is really very frightening.
Gertrude Stein

Gertrude Stein

Everybody gets so much information all day long that they lose their common sense. Gertrude Stein

Philosophy, like medicine, has plenty of drugs, few good remedies, and hardly any specific cures. Sebastien-Roch Nicolas de Chamfort

Truth is not hard to kill and a lie well told is immortal. Mark Twain

A lie can run around the world before the truth can get its boots on.
James Watt

James Watt

Obstacles are those frightful things we see when we take our eyes off our goal.
Henry Ford

The only sure thing about luck is that it will change.   Bret Harte

A wise man ought to realize that his health is his most reliable possession.
                                                                            Hippocrates

Do not draw the conclusion from your apprentice studies that you have nothing left to learn, but rather that you have infinitely more to learn.   Blaise Pascal

If space is, it will be in something; for everything that is is in something; and to be in something is to be in space, and so on (ad infinitum). Therefore space does not exist.   Zeno of Elea

The only good is knowledge and the only evil is ignorance.   Socrates

Socrates

As to gods, I have no way of knowing either that they exist or do not exist, or what they are like.   Protagoras of Abdera

Protagoras of Abdera

I know nothing except the fact of my ignorance.   Socrates

Conservatives are not necessarily stupid, but most stupid people are conservatives.
                                                                John Stuart Mill

If mankind minus one were of one opinion, then mankind is no more justified
in silencing the one than the one – if he had the power – would be justified in
silencing mankind.   John Stuart Mill

John Stuart Mill

No great improvements in the lot of mankind are possible until a great change
takes place in the fundamental constitution of their modes of thought.
                                                                John Stuart Mill

If everyone would give his best in his place, the world soon would improve a lot.
                                                                Adolph Kolping

Adolph Kolping

One person with a belief is equal to a force of 99 who have only interests.
                                                                John Stuart Mill

No one can be a great thinker who does not recognise that as a thinker it is his first duty to follow his intellect to whatever conclusions it may lead. Truth gains more even by the errors of one who, with due study, and preparation, thinks for himself, than by the true opinions of those who only hold them because they do not suffer themselves to think.   John Stuart Mill

A wise man once said, never discuss philosophy or politics in a disco environment.
                                                        Frank Zappa

The power of the lawyer is in the uncertainty of the law.   Jeremy Bentham

Certitude is impossible and only probable knowledge is attainable.
                                                        Pyrrhon of Elis

Pyrrhon of Elis

Whoever wants to reach a distant goal must take small steps.   Helmut Schmidt

Helmut Schmidt

Arriving at one goal is the starting point to another.   John Dewey

Success is dangerous. One begins to copy oneself, and to copy oneself is more dangerous than to copy others. It leads to sterility.   Pablo Picasso

Failure is instructive. The person who really thinks learns quite as much from his failures as from his successes.   John Dewey

Failure is only the opportunity to more intelligently begin again.   Henry Ford

I cannot give you the formula for success, but I can give you the formula for failure. Try to please everybody.   Herbert B. Swope

Without some goals and some efforts to reach it, no man can live.

John Dewey

A person without a sense of humour is like a wagon without springs. It's jolted by every pebble on the road.   Henry Ward Beecher

I will never deviate from truth, nobody will ever achieve that with me.

Ulrich von Hutten

Ulrich von Hutten

For a man to attain to an eminent degree in learning costs him time, watching, hunger, nakedness, dizziness in the head, weakness in the stomach, and other inconveniences.   Miguel de Cervantes Saavedra

From reading too much, and sleeping too little, his brain dried up on him and he lost his judgment.   Miguel de Cervantes Saavedra

I have never met a man so ignorant that I couldn't learn something from him.

Galileo Galilei

Human history becomes more and more a race between education and catastrophe.
Herbert George Wells

We only have the choice to learn by reason, or to be taught by catastrophes.
Hoimar von Ditfurth

Hoimar von Ditfurth

Men and nations behave wisely once they have exhausted all the other alternatives.
Abba Eban

I cannot think of the present state of humanity as that in which it is destined
to remain; I am absolutely unable to conceive of this as its complete and final
vocation. Only in so far as I can regard this state as the means towards a better,
as the transition-point to a higher and more perfect state, has it any value in my
eyes.   Johann Gottlieb Fichte

Johann Gottlieb Fichte

I want to stand as close to the edge as I can without going over. Out on the edge
you see all the kinds of things you can't see from the centre.   Kurt Vonnegut

Of all political ideas, perhaps the most dangerous is the wish to make people perfect and happy. The attempt to realise heaven on Earth has always produced a hell.   Sir Karl Popper

Genuine tragedies in the world are not conflicts between right and wrong. They are conflicts between two rights.   Georg Wilhelm Friedrich Hegel

Georg Wilhelm Friedrich Hegel

Religion is regarded by the common people as true, by the wise as false, and by the rulers as useful.   Seneca

Pure thought is itself the divine existence; and conversely, the divine existence, in its immediate essence, is nothing else than pure thought.
                                                              Johann Gottlieb Fichte

A new word is like a fresh seed sown on the ground of the discussion.
                                                              Ludwig Wittgenstein

God gives talent; work transforms it into genius.   Anna Pavlova

Mediocrity knows nothing higher than itself, but talent instantly recognises genius.   Sir Arthur Conan Doyle

The truth is rarely pure and never simple.   Oscar Wilde

What is true by lamplight is not always true by sunlight.   Joseph Joubert

Tell them the truth; first because it is the right thing to do and second they'll find out anyway.   John Wayne

Talk low, talk slow and don't say too much.   John Wayne

Nothing is often a good thing to do and always a good thing to say.

Will Durant

An army of deer lead by a lion is more to be feared than an army of lions lead by a deer.

Philip of Macedonia

Philip of Macedonia

[To the Spartans] "If I win this war, you will be slaves forever." [The Spartan's reply was laconic: "If".]

Philip of Macedonia

O how small a portion of earth will hold us when we are dead, who ambitiously seek after the whole world while we are living.

Philip of Macedonia

The production of too many useful things results in too many useless people.

Karl Marx

Karl Marx

Hope – deceptive though it may be, it leads us down a pleasant path through life.
Horst Janssen

Horst Janssen

In peace sons bury their fathers and in war the fathers bury their sons.
Francis Bacon

Francis Bacon

Between the idea and the reality, between the motion and the act falls the shadow.
Thomas Stearns Eliot

The ink of a scholar is more sacred that the blood of a martyr.   Mohammed

Intuition is the undoubting conception of a pure and attentive mind, which arises from the light of reason alone, and is more certain than deduction.
René Descartes

The more human beings proceed by plan the more effectively they may be hit by accident.   Friedrich Dürrenmatt

The greatest of all inventors is accident.   Marc Twain

A pessimist sees the difficulty in every opportunity; an optimist sees the opportunity in every difficulty.   Sir Winston Churchill

Sir Winston Churchill

To enjoy freedom we have to control ourselves.   Virginia Woolf

How often I have found that we grow to maturity not by doing what we like, but by doing what we should. How true it is that not every 'should' is a compulsion, and not every 'like' is a high morality and true freedom.   Karl Rahner

Karl Rahner

If our dreams were more regular, more connected, more stable, they would also have more practical importance for us.   Ernst Mach

Travel is ninety percent anticipation and ten percent recollection.

Edward Streeter

You will never 'find time' for anything. If you want time, you must make it.

Charles Buxton

It wasn't raining when Noah built the ark.   Howard Ruff

The greatest analgesic, soporific, stimulant, tranquiliser, narcotic, and to some extent even antibiotic – in short the closest thing to a genuine panacea known to medical science is work.   Thomas S. Szasz

A study of history shows that civilisations that abandon the quest for knowledge are doomed to disintegration.   Bernard Lovell

The greatest obstacle to discovery is not ignorance – it is the illusion of knowledge.   Daniel J. Boorstin

The salvation of mankind lies only in making everything the concern of all.
                                                    Alexander Solzhenitsyn

Alexander Solzhenitsyn

The illiterate of the 21st century will not be those who cannot read and write, but those who cannot learn, unlearn, and relearn.   Alvin Toffler

The man who never alters his opinions is like standing water, and breeds reptiles of the mind.   William Blake

Example is not the main thing in influencing others. It is the only thing.
                                                        Albert Schweitzer

To have doubted one's own first principles is the mark of a civilised man.
                                                    Oliver Wendell Holmes, Jr.

'Knowledge is power' is the finest idea ever put into words.   Ernest J. Renan

Knowledge, to become wisdom, needs judgement.
                                            Lord Samuel Richard Attenborough

The kind of world we live in tomorrow depends, not partially, but entirely upon the type and quality of the education of our children today.   Martin Vanbee

Education is the most powerful weapon which you can use to change the world.
Nelson Mandela

It is an educated barbarian who is worst; he knows what to destroy.
Helen MacInnes

Just as philosophy is the study of other people's misconceptions, so history is the study of other people's mistakes.   Phillip Guedala

All philosophies, if you ride them home, are nonsense, but some are greater non-sense than others.   Samuel Butler

The most dangerous criminal now is the entirely lawless modern philosopher. Compared to him, burglars and bigamists are essentially moral men.
Gilbert Keith Chesterton

There is no statement so absurd that no philosopher will make it.   Cicero

If a million people believe a foolish thing, it is still a foolish thing.
Anatole France

Anatole France

A learned fool is more foolish than an ignorant fool.   Molière

It is what we think we know already that often prevents us from learning.
Claude Bernard

All truth passes through three stages. First, it is ridiculed. Second, it is violently opposed. Third, it is accepted as being self-evident.   Arthur Schopenhauer

Arthur Schopenhauer

The skeptic being a lover of his kind, desires to cure by speech, as best he can, the self-conceit and rashness of the dogmatists. So, just as the physicians who cure bodily ailments have remedies which differ in strength, and apply the severe ones to those whose ailments are severe and the milder to those mildly affected – so too the skeptic propounds arguments which differ in strength, and employs those which are weighty and capable by their stringency of disposing of the dogmatists' ailment, self-conceit, in cases where the mischief is due to a severe attack of rashness, which he employs the milder arguments in the case of those whose ailment is superficial and easy to cure, and whom it is possible to restore to health by milder methods of persuasion.   Sextus Empiricus

Sextus Empiricus

Perfect Scepticisme is a disease incurable, and a thing rather to be pitied or laughed at, then seriously opposed. For when a man is so fugitive and unsettled that he will not stand to the verdict of his own Faculties, one can no more fasten any thing upon him, than he can write in the water, or tye knots in the wind.

Henry More

Henry More

The seeker after truth is not one who studies the writings of the ancients and, following his natural disposition, puts his trust in them, but, rather, the one who suspects his faith in them and questions what he gathers from them, the one who submits to argument and demonstration.   Abu Ali Al-Hasan Ibn Al-Haitham

The height of cleverness is to be able to conceal it.

François de La Rochefoucauld

Genius does not obey the rules – it makes them.   Michael Ghiselin

A little learning is a dangerous thing but none at all is fatal.   Roger Bacon

The roots of education are bitter, but the fruit is sweet.   Aristotle

Education without cheering up is only half of the story.   Peter Sloterdijk

Anyone who stops learning is old, whether at twenty or eighty. Anyone who keeps learning stays young. The greatest thing in life is to keep your mind young.

Henry Ford

Life means suffering: birth is suffering, aging is suffering, illness is suffering, death is suffering.   Buddha

You philosophers are lucky men. You write on paper and paper is patient. Unfortunate Empress that I am, I write on the susceptible skins of living beings.

Catherine the Great

Catherine the Great

The noble truth of the origin of suffering: it is this craving which leads to renewed existence, accompanied by delight and lust, seeking delight here and there, that is, craving for sensual pleasures, craving for existence, craving for extermination.

Buddha

The noble truth of the cessation of suffering: it is the remainderless fading away and cessation of that same craving, the giving up and relinquishing of it, freedom from it, nonreliance on it.   Buddha

The noble truth of the way leading to the cessation of suffering: it is the Noble Eightfold Path; that is, right view, right intention, right speech, right action, right livelihood, right effort, right mindfulness, right concentration.   Buddha

Psychiatry's chief contribution to philosophy is the discovery that the toilet is the seat of the soul.   Alexander Chase

If the human mind were simple enough to understand, we'd be too simple to understand it.   Pat Bahn

If the human brain were so simple that we could understand it, we would be so simple that we couldn't.   Emerson M. Pugh
(also attributed to Lyall Watson)

The mind is like an iceberg, it floats with one-seventh of its bulk above water.

Sigmund Freud

Sigmund Freud

There is not past, no future; everything flows in an eternal present.

James Joyce

Nations have their ego, just like individuals.   James Joyce

James Joyce

Learn the rules so that you can break them.   Dalai Lama

If one does not understand a person, one tends to regard him as a fool.

Carl Gustav Jung

Mental health problems do not affect three or four out of every five persons but one out of one.   William Menninger

Anybody who is 25 or 30 years old has physical scars from all sorts of things, from tuberculosis to polio. It's the same with the mind.   Moses R. Kaufman

The conscious mind may be compared to a fountain playing in the sun and falling back into the great subterranean pool of subconscious from which it rises.

                                                                    Sigmund Freud

I believe in everything until it's disproved. So I believe in fairies, the myths, dragons. It all exists, even if it's in your mind. Who's to say that dreams and nightmares aren't as real as the here and now?   John Lennon

John Lennon

Dreams are the best proof that we are not so strongly enclosed in our skin as it appears.   Friedrich Hebbel

Friedrich Hebbel

The spirit of Plato dies hard. We have been unable to escape the philosophical tradition that what we can see and measure in the world is merely the superficial and imperfect representation of an underlying reality.   Stephen Jay Gould

Plato, by the way, wanted to banish all poets from his proposed Utopia because they were liars. The truth was that Plato knew philosophers couldn't compete successfully with poets.   Kilgore Trout

Nothing is more astounding than the truth, nothing more exotic than our environment, and nothing is more fantastic than reality ...   Egon Erwin Kisch

Egon Erwin Kisch

Be not astonished at new ideas; for it is well known to you that a thing does not therefore cease to be true because it is not accepted by many.   Baruch Spinoza

Reality is that which, when you stop believing in it, doesn't go away.
                                                                Philip K. Dick

Facts do not cease to exist because they are ignored.   Aldous Huxley

A free society is one where it is safe to be unpopular.   Adlai Stevenson

Any philosophy that can be put in a nutshell belongs there.   Sydney J. Harris

Any two philosophers can tell each other all they know in two hours.
                                                    Oliver Wendell Holmes, Jr.

Philosophers dwell in the moon.   John Ford

Cogito ergo I'm right and you're wrong.   Blair Houghton

Common sense is instinct, and enough of it is genius.   Josh Billings

Common sense is the collection of prejudices acquired by age eighteen.

Albert Einstein

Common sense is not so common.   Voltaire

A great many people think they are thinking when they are merely rearranging their prejudices.   William James

The only reason some people get lost in thought is because it's unfamiliar territory.

Paul Fix

Ours is a world of nuclear giants and ethical infants.

General Omar N. Bradley

There are more things in heaven and earth, Horatio, than are dreamt of in your philosophy.   William Shakespeare [Hamlet]

William Shakespeare

I have made this letter longer than usual because I lack the time to make it shorter.

Blaise Pascal

Thanks to the acuteness of his mind, he saw through the poverty of philosophical and Gnostic knowledge, and contemptuously rejected it.   Carl Gustav Jung

The only thing we learn from history is that we learn nothing from history.

Georg Wilhelm Friedrich Hegel

Writing about music is like dancing about architecture.   Frank Zappa

A self does not amount to much, but no self is an island; each exists in a fabric of relations that is now more complex and mobile than ever before.

Jean-François Lyotard

The human soul can look either upward or downward; up to the sphere of purer spirit, or down to the evil regions of matter.   Plotinus

Plotinus

He who knows nothing is closer to the truth than he whose mind is filled with falsehoods and errors.   Thomas Jefferson

Rational knowledge is a cognition of intelligible realities, or Ideas in the realm of Mind which is often referred to as Divine.   Plotinus

A man's errors are his portals of discovery.   James Joyce

Generally speaking, the errors in religion are dangerous; those in philosophy only ridiculous.   David Hume

David Hume

Religions must serve humanity, not the other way around.   Dalai Lama

Humanity finds itself in the midst of the world. In the midst of all other creatures humanity is the most significant and yet the most dependent upon the others.

Hildegard of Bingen

Esse est percipi (To be is to be perceived).   George Berkeley

Everything is relative.   Epimenides

Epimenides

All the choir of Heaven and furniture of Earth – in a word, all those bodies which compose the frame of the world – have not any subsistence without a mind.

George Berkeley

I close my eyes in order to see.   Anthonis van Dyck

Anthonis van Dyck

A mind all logic is like a knife all blade. It makes the hand bleed that uses it.

Rabindranath Tagore

It's exactly where a thought is lacking, That, just in time, a word shows up instead.

Johann Wolfgang von Goethe

I must tell you that the supply of words on the world market is plentiful, but the demand is falling.

Lech Walesa

Lech Walesa

We cannot appeal to the conscience of the world when our own conscience is asleep.

Carl von Ossietzky

3.3 Soul

A year spent in artificial intelligence is enough to make one believe in God.

Alan J. Perlis

For who among men is he that can know the counsel of God? or who can think what the will of God is?   Salomo, The Book of Wisdom, 9.13

And indeed we believe you [God] to be something than which a greater cannot be conceived.   Anselm of Canterbury

Anselm of Canterbury

There is no evil in the atom; only in men's souls.   Adlai Stevenson

If you're losing your soul and you know it, then you've still got a soul left to lose.

Charles Bukowski

What shall it profit a man if he gains the whole world but loses his soul.

Jesus Christ

Jesus Christ

If vacillation dwell with the heart the soul will rue it.

Wolfram von Eschenbach

Television is as injurious to the soul as fast food is to the body.   Quentin Crisp

Quentin Crisp

Looking back over the geological record it would seem that Nature made nearly every possible mistake before she reached her greatest achievement. Man – or perhaps some would say her worst mistake of all. ... At last she tried a being of no great size, almost defenseless, defective in at least one of the more important sense organs; one gift she bestowed to save him from threatened extinction – a certain stirring, a restlessness, in the organ called the brain.

Sir Arthur Eddington

We all dance to a mysterious tune, intoned in the distance by an invisible player.

Albert Einstein

We are a bit of stellar matter gone wrong. We are physical machinery – puppets that strut and talk and laugh and die as the hand of time pulls the strings beneath. But there is one elementary inescapable answer. We are that which asks the question.   Sir Arthur Eddington

I like to browse in occult bookshops if for no other reason than to refresh my commitment to science.   Heinz R. Pagels

I cannot walk through the suburbs in the solitude of the night without thinking that the night pleases us because it suppresses idle details, just as our memory does.   Jorge Luis Borges

Night, the beloved. Night, when words fade and things come alive. When the destructive analysis of day is done, and all that is truly important becomes whole and sound again. When man reassembles his fragmentary self and grows with the calm of a tree.   Antoine de Saint-Exupéry

Physics may serve the philosopher as a weapon against the uninitiated who ridicule the holiness of science into which they cannot reach.   Hans Christian Oersted

Hans Christian Oersted

Don't go outside. Look inside yourself. The truth lies on the inside.
                                                                    St. Augustine

"The stars are made of the same atoms as the earth." I usually pick one small topic like this to give a lecture on. Poets say science takes away from the beauty of the stars – mere gobs of gas atoms. Nothing is 'mere'. I too can see the stars on a desert night, and feel them. But do I see less or more? The vastness of the heavens stretches my imagination – stuck on this carousel my little eye can catch one-million-year-old light. A vast pattern – of which I am a part – perhaps my stuff was belched from some forgotten star, as one is belching there. Or see them with the greater eye of Palomar, rushing all apart from some common starting point when they were perhaps all together. What is the pattern, or the meaning, or the *why*? It does not do harm to the mystery to know a little about it. For far more marvelous is the truth than any artists of the past imagined! Why do the poets of the present not speak of it? What men are poets who can speak of Jupiter if he were like a man, but if he is an immense spinning sphere of methane and ammonia must be silent?   Richard P. Feynman

It seems to me that nearly every woman I know wants a man who knows how to love with authority. Women are simple souls who like simple things, and one of the simplest is one of the simplest to give. ... Our family Airedale will come clear across the yard for one pat on the head. The average wife is like that.

Episcopal Bishop James Pike

Judge me for my own merits, or lack of them, but do not look upon me as a mere appendage to this great general or that great scholar, this star that shines at the court of France or that famed author [she speaks of the great Voltaire]. I am in my own right a whole person, responsible to myself alone for all that I am, all that I say, all that I do. It may be that there are metaphysicians and philosophers whose learning is greater than mine, although I have not met them. Yet, they are but frail humans, too, and have their faults; so, when I add the sum total of my graces, I confess I am inferior to no one. [In a letter to Frederick the Great of Prussia]

Emilie du Châtelét

Emilie du Châtelét

The main difference between men and women is that men are lunatics and women are idiots.

Rebecca West

Whether women are better than men I cannot say – but I can say they are certainly no worse.

Golda Meir

I cannot see that the gender of a candidate can be an argument against acceptance. After all we are not a public swimming bath.

Quotation by David Hilbert during a faculty meeting about the acceptance of Emmy Noether concerning the position of a lecturer

Her heart knew no malice, she did not believe in evil – indeed it never entered her mind that it could play a role among men. [About Emmy Noether]

Hermann Weyl

Emmy Noether

I like your Christ, but I do not like your Christians because they are too unlike your Christ.   Mahatma Gandhi

Mahatma Gandhi

Bach almost persuades me to become a Christian.   Roger Fry

The Christian of the future will be a mystic or he will not exist at all.

Karl Rahner

My religion consists of a humble admiration of the illimitable superior spirit who reveals himself in the slight details we are able to perceive with our frail and feeble minds.   Albert Einstein

There are many religions, but there is only one morality.   John Ruskin

The work will wait while you show the child the rainbow, but the rainbow won't wait while you do the work.   Joan O'Hara

If you want your children to turn out well, spend twice as much time with them as you think you should and half the amount of money.   Esther Selsdon

All that a husband or wife really wants is to be pitied a little, praised a little, appreciated a little.   Oliver Goldsmith

As a cure for worrying, work is better than whiskey.   Thomas Alva Edison

I like work; it fascinates me. I can sit and look at it for hours.

Jerome K. Jerome

Jerome K. Jerome

It is the quality of our work which will please God and not the quantity.

Mahatma Gandhi

The secret is keeping busy, and loving what you do.   Lionel Hampton

Inspiration could be called inhaling the memory of an act never experienced.

Ned Rorem

Leisure is the mother of philosophy.   Thomas Hobbes

If you are losing your leisure, look out, you may be losing your soul.

Logan Pearsall Smith

We must learn to be still in the midst of activity and to be vibrantly alive in repose.
Indira Gandhi

The most important thing in communication is to hear what isn't been said.
Peter F. Drucker

Great minds discuss ideas. Average minds discuss events. Small minds discuss.
Eleanor Roosevelt

Eleanor Roosevelt

To talk well and eloquently is a very great art, but an equally great one is to know
the right moment to stop.   Wolfgang Amadeus Mozart

Wolfgang Amadeus Mozart

One of the penalties for refusing to participate in politics is that you end up being governed by your inferiors.   Plato

Are quarks and gluons the Platonic ideas of commonly observed objects?
                                                     Claus Grupen

Everything that is really great and inspiring is created by the individual who can labor in freedom.   Albert Einstein

Personal freedom is the most important resource of mankind.   Florian Geyer

Florian Geyer

Monarchy is the gold filling in the mouth of decay.   John Osborne

Life must be understood backwards; but ... it must be lived forward.
                                                  Søren Kierkegaard

A path needs no where to, a where from is sufficient.   Ernst Barlach

Ernst Barlach

Youth is happy because it has the ability to see beauty. Anyone who keeps the ability to see beauty never grows old.   Franz Kafka

There is not one blade of grass, there is no color in this world that is not intended
to make us rejoice.   John Calvin

The happiest marriages are full of alternative lives, lived in the head, unknown to
the partner.   John Bayley

Eternity is a mere moment, just long enough for a joke.   Hermann Hesse

Hermann Hesse

I can grasp now the idea of eternity, but infinity is still beyond me.
                                                                    Claus Grupen

He who has no vision of eternity will never get a true hold of time.
                                                                  Thomas Carlyle

The more determinedly I exist, as myself, within the conditions of the time, the
more clearly I shall hear the language of the past, the nearer I shall feel the glow
of its life.   Karl Theodor Jaspers

Karl Theodor Jaspers

A man endures misfortune without complaint.   Franz Schubert

Franz Schubert

In essentials, unity; in differences, liberty; in all things, charity.

Philipp Melanchthon

Philipp Melanchthon

Anticipate charity by preventing poverty.   Maimonides (Moshe Ben Maimon)

See everything, overlook a great deal, correct a little.   Pope John XXIII

Riches and power are but gifts of blind fate, whereas goodness is the result of one's own merits.   Héloïse

Tolerance does not require to camouflage differences and inconsistencies. On the contrary, it asks for accepting that a comprehensive universal thinking is impossible. Therefore, different and contradicting points of view must be acknowledged without hatred and hostility.   Lew Sinowjewitsch Kopelew

Lew Sinowjewitsch Kopelew

As the archaeology of our thought easily shows, man is an invention of recent date. And one perhaps nearing its end.   Michel Foucault

A countryman between two lawyers is like a fish between two cats.
                    Benjamin Franklin

Genius can probably run on ahead and seek out new ways. But the good artists who follow after genius – and I count myself among these – have to restore the lost connection once more.   Käthe Kollwitz

Käthe Kollwitz

Life is unfair but remember: sometimes it is unfair in your favour.
                    Peter Ustinov

Living is like licking honey off a thorn.   Louis Adamic

A mind that is characterised by unrest will not tranquil even in the presence of great calm.
Dalai Lama

Smile if you want a smile from another face.
Dalai Lama

I must study politics and war that my sons may have liberty to study mathematics and philosophy. My sons ought to study mathematics and philosophy, geography, natural history, naval architecture, navigation, commerce and agriculture in order to give their children a right to study painting, poetry, music, architecture, statuary, tapestry, and porcelain.
John Adams

Whatever you do will be insignificant, but it is very important that you do it.
Mahatma Gandhi

The darkest places in hell are reserved for those who maintain their neutrality in times of moral crisis.
Dante Alighieri

Who fails to do something, is not free of debt. Nobody retains his virginity by being passive.
Siegfried Lenz

Siegfried Lenz

In the crisis the character becomes evident.
Helmut Schmidt

To have character means to stand to the thousand errors, which one has made in the course of ones life.
Alexander Mitscherlich

The society which scorns excellence in plumbing because plumbing is a humble activity, and tolerates shoddiness in philosophy because philosophy is an exalted activity, will have neither good plumbing nor good philosophy. Neither its pipes nor its theories will hold water.
John W. Gardner

The less people know about how sausages and laws are made, the better they'll
sleep at night.   Fürst Otto von Bismarck

There will be no end to the troubles of states, or of humanity itself, till philosophers become kings in this world, or till those we now call kings and rulers really
and truly become philosophers, and political power and philosophy thus come into
the same hands.   Plato

Far too many people do not understand to keep the necessary philosophical distance to the world – particularly in Germany, the romping place of obtrusive diligence, they don't understand this. And that is a pity, because they miss the powerful wellspring, a refreshment which cannot be compared to anything else.
                                                                       Kurt Kusenberg

Kurt Kusenberg

When he who hears does not know what he who speaks means, and when he who
speaks does not know what he himself means, that is philosophy.   Voltaire

Hear much; speak little.   Bias of Priene

First learn the meaning of what you say, and then speak.   Epictetus

Listen to many, speak to a few.   William Shakespeare

Politeness is the art of choosing among your thoughts.   Madame de Staël

Art is the daughter of freedom.   Friedrich Schiller

Every science begins as philosophy and ends as art.   Will Durant

Facts can be turned into art if one is artful enough.   Paul Simon

Religion is the everlasting dialogue between humanity and God. Art is its soliloquy.
                                                                    Franz Werfel

Franz Werfel

Humanity today possesses sufficient economic, cultural and spiritual resources to introduce a better global order.   Hans Küng

Were there none who were discontented with what they have, the world would never reach anything better.   Florence Nightingale

There is no worse screen to block out the Spirit than confidence in our own intelligence.   John Calvin

Science without religion is lame, religion without science is blind.
                                                                 Albert Einstein

A little science leads you away from God. A lot of it guides you back to him.
                                                              Antoine de Rivarol
                           (also attributed to Marcel Proust and Louis Pasteur)

Logic is one thing, the human animal another. You can quite easily propose a logical solution to something and at the same time hope in your heart of hearts it won't work out.   Luigi Pirandello

Painting is the grandchild of Nature. It is related to God.   Rembrandt

Practise what you know, and it will help to make clear what now you do not know.
                                                                    Rembrandt

I inherited a painting and a violin which turned out to be a Rembrandt and a Stradivarius. Unfortunately, Rembrandt made lousy violins and Stradivarius was a terrible painter.   Tommy Cooper

Choose only one master – Nature.   Rembrandt

Rembrandt

My advice to you is not to inquire why or whither, but just enjoy your ice cream while it's on your plate – that's my philosophy.   Thornton Wilder

The only thing that we know is that we know nothing and that is the highest flight of human wisdom.   Leo Tolstoy

Leo Tolstoy

He who knows best knows how little he knows.   Thomas Jefferson

Dive into the sea of thought, and find there pearls beyond price.

Moses Ibn Ezra

It was previously a question of finding out whether or not life had to have a meaning to be lived. It now becomes clear, on the contrary, that it will be lived all the better if it has no meaning.   Albert Camus

To think and to be fully alive are the same.   Hannah Arendt

Those who love something passionately are more likely to be right than those who
don't.   Yehudi Menuhin

I don't want to achieve immortality through my work. I want to achieve immortality by not dying.   Woody Allen

Do not walk through time without leaving memorable evidence of your passage.
                                                                        Karl Riha

Karl Riha

The longer you look at an object, the more abstract it becomes, and, ironically, the
more real.   Lucian Freud

Lucian Freud

I adore art … when I am alone with my notes, my heart pounds and the tears stream from my eyes, and my emotion and my joys are too much to bear.

Giuseppe Verdi

Giuseppe Verdi

The purpose of art is not the momentary ejection of adrenaline, but rather the lifelong construction of a state of wonder and serenity. Glenn Gould

Glenn Gould

How a person masters his fate is more important than what his fate is.

Wilhelm von Humboldt

A room without books is like a body without a soul. Cicero

Bookshops are centres for civilisation. Rebecca West

A second-hand bookshop is the sign and symbol of a civilised community and the number and quality of these shops give you the exact measure of a city's right to be counted among the great cities of the world. Walter Murdoch

The best doctors in the world are Doctor Diet, Doctor Quiet and Doctor Merry-
man.   Jonathan Swift

Get married, in any case. If you happen to get a good mate, you will be happy; if
a bad one, you will become philosophical, which is a fine thing in itself.

                                                                      Socrates

Ask yourself whether you are happy and you cease to be so.   John Stuart Mill

John Stuart Mill

Let us stay brave and always get more soft-gloved and happier for these few days
on Earth.   Detlev von Liliencron

Detlev von Liliencron

He uses statistics as a drunken man uses lampposts – for support rather than for
illumination.   Andre Lang

No human being will ever know the truth, for even if they happen to say it by chance, they would not even known they had done so.

Xenophanes

Dogmatism is a fault in character.

Pyrrhon of Elis

He who loses gold or silver can find more to replace it, but he who loses time cannot find more.

Monks and nuns of the Egyptian desert

The two things which, of all others, most want to be under strict rule, and which are the greatest blessings to ourselves and others, when they are rightly used, are our time and our money.

William Law

It is strange that the years teach us patience; that the shorter our time, the greater our capacity for waiting.

Elizabeth Taylor

Spend some time alone every day.

Dalai Lama

Thousands of candles can be lit from a single candle, and the life of the candle will not be shortened. Happiness never decreases by being shared.

Buddha

Every wave, regardless of how high and forceful it crests, must eventually collapse within itself.

Stefan Zweig

A line is a dot that went for a walk.

Paul Klee

Paul Klee

Art does not reproduce the visible; rather, it makes visible.

Paul Klee

A good artist dips his brush in his own soul, and paints his own imagination, nature and desires into his pictures.   Lucas Cranach the Elder

Lucas Cranach the Elder

The true work of art is but a shadow of the divine perfection.

Michelangelo Buonarroti

Michelangelo Buonarroti

Beauty is no quality in things themselves: it exists merely in the mind which contemplates them.   David Hume

Beauty is not caused. It is.   Emily Dickinson

The first question I ask myself when something doesn't seem to be beautiful is why do I think it's not beautiful. And very shortly you discover that there is no reason.   John Cage

It is the path of least resistance that makes rivers and men crooked.

Bartlett Joshua Palmer

If you believe everything you read, better not read.   Japanese proverb

Japanese nobleman

Everything has been said, only not by everyone.   Karl Valentin

It is certain that nothing is certain, therefore, as a precaution, I mistrust everything.

Karl Valentin

Karl Valentin

I reject the philosophy that if you eliminate the impossible, whatever remains, no matter how improbably, must be the truth. The impossible often has a kind of integrity which the merely improbable lacks.   Douglas Adams

In order to attain the impossible, one must attempt the absurd.

Miguel de Cervantes Saavedra

Philosophy is just a hobby. You can't open a philosophy factory.

Dewey Selmon

Being a philosopher, I have a problem for every solution.   Robert Zend

The point of philosophy is to start with something so simple as not to seem worth stating, and to end with something so paradoxical that no one will believe it.

Bertrand A. W. Russell

Because philosophy arises from awe, a philosopher is bound in his way to be a lover of myths and poetic fables. Poets and philosophers are alike in being big with wonder.   St. Thomas Aquinas

There is only one thing a philosopher can be relied upon to do, and that is to contradict other philosophers.   William James

There is no record in human history of a happy philosopher.

Henry Louis Mencken

If we behave differently we will get different answers.   Samy Molcho

Samy Molcho

You can never lose what you never had.   Dican (a fancy Naruto TV figure)

An object in possession seldom retains the same charm that it had in pursuit.

Plinius the Younger

There is no great genius without some touch of madness.   Seneca

It takes a lot of time to be a genius, you have to sit around so much doing nothing, really doing nothing.   Gertrude Stein

Genius is nothing but a greater aptitude for patience.   Georges de Buffon

Georges Louis le Clerc, Comte de Buffon

There is a very narrow line between a madman and a genius: They meet on the other side.   Claus Grupen

Genius means little more than the faculty of perceiving in an unhabitual way.
                                                                         William James

Toleration is the greatest gift of the mind; it requires the same effort of the brain that it takes to balance oneself on a bicycle.   Helen Keller

The brain is wider than the sky.   Emily Dickinson

Any man who reads too much and uses his own brain too little falls into lazy habits of thinking.   Albert Einstein

God designed the stomach to eject what is bad for it, but the human brain works differently.   Konrad Adenauer

The second (of Zeno of Elea's arguments about motion) is the one called 'Achilles'. This is to the effect that the slowest as it runs will never be caught by the quickest. For the pursuer must first reach the point from which the pursued departed, so that the slower must always be some distance in front.   Aristotle

Death may be the greatest of all human blessings.   Socrates

Socrates

After your death you will be what you were before your birth.
                                                    Arthur Schopenhauer

Humans are the only living beings which know that they will eventually die. The
suppression of this knowledge is the only and main calamity of humans.
                                                    Friedrich Dürrenmatt

What you leave behind is not what is engraved in stone monuments, but what is
woven into the lives of others.   Pericles

Pericles

European imperialism long ago made Tahiti a distant suburb of Paris, the missionaries made it a suburb of Christ's kingdom, and the radio made it a suburb of Los Angeles.   Cedric Belfrage

Tahiti

In a rich man's house there is no place to spit but his face.   Diogenes

It is the wretchedness of being rich that you have to live with rich people.
                                                                                            Logan Pearsall Smith

He has the most who is most content with the least.   Diogenes

Who is rich? He that is content. Who is that? Nobody.   Benjamin Franklin

If Karl, instead of writing a lot about capital, had made a lot of it, it would have been much better.   Karl Marx' mother

Great abundance of riches cannot be gathered and kept by any man without sin.
                                                                                            Erasmus of Rotterdam

It is easier for a camel to pass through the eye of a needle than for a rich man to enter the Kingdom of Heaven.   Jesus Christ

If you would know what the Lord God thinks of money, you have only to look at those to whom He gives it.   Maurice Baring

If you want to know what god thinks of money, just look at the people he gave it to.   Dorothy Parker

It is neither wealth nor splendour, but tranquillity and occupation, which give happiness.   Thomas Jefferson

The writing of the wise are the only riches our posterity cannot squander.
                                                                                            Walter Savage Landor

Philosophy triumphs easily over past evils and future evils; but present evils triumph over it.   François de La Rochefoucauld

When we are tired, we are attacked by ideas we conquered long ago.
                                                        Friedrich Nietzsche

Friedrich Nietzsche

A day without sunshine is, you know, night.   Powell Shannon

Love takes up where knowledge leaves off.   St. Thomas Aquinas

Gravitation is not responsible for people falling in love.   Albert Einstein

Religion has done love a great service by making it a sin.   Anatole France

Everywhere, we learn only from those whom we love.
                                                Johann Wolfgang von Goethe

Johann Wolfgang von Goethe

If information is not knowledge. Knowledge is not wisdom. Wisdom is not truth. Truth is not beauty. Beauty is not love. Love is not music. Music is THE BEST.

Frank Zappa

Anything that is too stupid to be spoken is sung. Voltaire

Music is always noise-related, and often not appreciated. Wilhelm Busch

Wilhelm Busch

Without music life would be a mistake. Friedrich Nietzsche

Music in the soul can be heard by the universe. Lao-Tzu

Red wine is the lubricant of the old man's soul. Claus Grupen

Wine is bottled poetry. Robert Louis Stevenson

A whisky for breakfast? It takes off the high frequencies! Stirling Colgate

The key source for humour originates from suffering, from defeats.

Friedrich Karl Waechter

Friedrich Karl Waechter

Humor is in fact an essential element in the mirth of creation. We can see how, in many matters in our lives, God wants to prod us into taking things a bit more lightly.   Pope Benedict XVI

Pope Benedict XVI

If there were no God there would be no atheists.   Gilbert Keith Chesterton

I cannot say whether things will get better if we change; what I can say is they must change if they are to get better.   Georg Christoph Lichtenberg

God created man in His own image, says the Bible; philosophers reverse the process: they create God in theirs.   Georg Christoph Lichtenberg

mediaeval student

The Devil's cleverest ploy is to persuade you that he doesn't exist.

Charles Baudelaire

Mendicant orders and monks have been imagined and contrived by the devil.

Jan Hus

Jan Hus

In heaven all the interesting people are missing.   Friedrich Nietzsche

We may be surprised at the people we find in heaven. God has a soft spot for sinners. His standards are quite low.   Bishop Desmond Tutu

Thousands have gone to heaven who have never read one page of the Bible.

Francis A. Baker

To be a philosophical skeptic is, in a man of letters, the first and most essential to being a sound, believing Christian.   David Hume

Atheism is easy in fair weather.   Ronald Dunn

Let us not be too hasty in judging the Devil. It must be remembered that we have heard only one side of the case, God has written all the books.   Samuel Butler

It is my ambition to say in ten sentences what others say in a whole book.

Friedrich Nietzsche

Change alone is eternal, perpetual, immortal.   Arthur Schopenhauer

And soon, too soon, we part with pain, To sail o'er silent seas again.

Thomas Moore

True change takes place in the imagination.   Thomas Moore

Thomas Moore

You can go wherever you want, you never come back the way you were.
                                                                   Siegfried Lenz

If you can spend a perfectly useless afternoon in a perfectly useless manner, you
have learned to live.   Lin Yutang

The greatest mistake you can make in life is to be continually fearing you will
make one.   Elbert Green Hubbard

The truest health is to be able to get on without it.   Robert Louis Stevenson

Everything has been figured out, except how to live.   Jean-Paul Sartre

Jean-Paul Sartre

For the sake of making a living, men forget to live.   Margaret Fuller

Start by doing what is necessary, then what's possible and suddenly you're doing
the impossible.   St. Francis of Assisi

We are masters of the unsaid words, but slaves of those we let slip out.

Sir Winston Churchill

Believe those who are seeking the truth. Doubt those who say they have found
it.   André Gide

There is absolutely no criterion for truth. For reason, senses, ideas, or whatever
else may exist are all deceptive.   Carneades of Cyrene

Carneades of Cyrene

People who want to share their religious views with you almost never want you to
share yours with them.   Dave Berry

A long dispute means that both parties are wrong.   Bob Phillips

Perhaps the straight and narrow path would be wider if more people used it.

Kay Ingram

Everyone is a moon and has a dark side which he never shows to anybody.

Mark Twain

If a man can remember what he worried about last week, he has a very good
memory.   Woody Allen

The world is not a place where good is rewarded and evil is punished.

Colin Douglas Semper

The best is the enemy of the good.   Voltaire

Lord, make me an instrument of your peace; where there is hatred, let me sow love; where there is injury, pardon; where there is doubt, faith; where there is despair, hope; where there is darkness, light; and where there is sadness, joy.

St. Francis of Assisi

St. Francis of Assisi

A thing moderately good is not so good as it ought to be. Moderation in temper is always a virtue, but moderation in principle is always a vice.   Thomas Paine

Laws are spider webs through which the big flies pass and the little ones get caught.   Honoré de Balzac

Honoré de Balzac

Right is right even if nobody does it. Wrong is wrong even if everybody is wrong about it.   Gilbert Keith Chesterton

The more laws and order are made prominent, the more thieves and robbers there will be.
                                                                            Lao-Tzu

Any crooked bookkeeper's books are balanced.   James Ferguson

It is easier to resist at the beginning than at the end.   Leonardo da Vinci

The truth of the matter is that you always know the right thing to do. The hard part is doing it.   Norman Schwarzkopf

To see and listen to the wicked is already the beginning of wickedness.
                                                                            Confucius

No snowflake in the avalanche ever feels responsible.   Stanislaw Jerzy Lec

The only people who are never converted to spiritualism are conjurers.
                                                                            George Orwell

George Orwell

This is the way the world ends
Not with a bang but a whimper.   Thomas Stearns Eliot

In our time this search for extraterrestrial life will eventually change our laws, our religions, our philosophies, our arts, our recreations, as well as our sciences. Space, the mirror, waits for life to come look for itself there.   Ray Bradbury

Worry is interest paid on trouble before it comes due.   William Ralph Inge

The family is one of Nature's masterpieces.   George Santayana

Our love for our children springs from the soul's greatest yearning for immortality.
                                                                            Plato

The problem with people who have no vices is that generally you can be pretty sure they're going to have some pretty annoying virtues.   Elizabeth Taylor

Elizabeth Taylor

How wise are thy commandments, Lord. Each of them applies to someone I know.
                                                            Sam Levenson

No people do so much harm as those who go about doing good.
                                                        Mandell Creighton

If you would be a real seeker after truth, it is necessary that at least once in your life you doubt, as far as possible, all things.   René Descartes

The eye sees what it is looking for.   Max Slevogt

Max Slevogt

Perfect numbers like perfect men are very rare.   René Descartes

It is one of the chief skills of the philosopher not to occupy himself with questions
which do not concern him.   Ludwig Wittgenstein

Ludwig Wittgenstein

The superfluous is very necessary.   Voltaire

The time you enjoy wasting is not wasted time.   Bertrand A. W. Russell

It is better to waste one's youth than to do nothing with it at all.
                                                                     Georges Courteline

In fact, sensations of pleasure and pain, however faint they may be, really consti-
tute an essential part of the content of all so-called emotions.   Ernst Mach

Ernst Mach

Being published by the Oxford University Press is rather like being married to a
duchess; the honour is greater than the pleasure.   George Malcolm Young

If the whole human race lay in one grave, the epitaph on its headstone might well
be: "It seemed a good idea at the time."   Rebecca West

A hero is someone who understands the responsibility that comes with his freedom.
                                                        Bob Dylan

Insanity in individuals is rare – but in groups, parties, nations, and epochs, it is the rule.
                                                 Friedrich Nietzsche

What difference does it make to the dead, the orphans and the homeless, whether the mad destruction is wrought under the name of totalitarianism or the holy body of liberty and democracy?
                                                   Mahatma Gandhi

What a lot we lost when we stopped writing letters. You cannot reread a phone call.
                                                     Liz Carpenter

The man of science is a poor philosopher.   Albert Einstein

The secret of teaching is to appear to have known all your life what you learned only yesterday.
                                                        John Burns

Good teaching is one-fourth preparation and three-fourth theatre.
                                                       Gail Godwin

The highest education is that which does not merely give us information but makes our life in harmony with all existence.
                                            Rabindranath Tagore

Education is an admirable thing, but it is well to remember from time to time that nothing that is worth knowing can be taught.
                                                       Oscar Wilde

Beware of the man of one book.   St. Thomas Aquinas

St. Thomas Aquinas

Philosophy, rightly defined, is simply the love of wisdom.
                                              Marcus Tullius Cicero

I have studied many philosophers and many cats. The wisdom of cats is infinitely superior.
                                                    Hippolyte Taine

There is a wisdom of the head, and a wisdom of the heart.   Charles Dickens

Experience has shown, and a true philosophy will always show, that a vast, perhaps the larger portion of the truth arises from the seemingly irrelevant.

Edgar Allen Poe

Edgar Allen Poe

By the time a man realises that maybe his father was right, he usually has a son who thinks he's wrong.   Charles Wadsworth

Clever people master life; the wise illuminate it and create fresh difficulties.

Emil Nolde

Emil Nolde

A wise man speaks because he has something to say; a fool because he has to say something.   Plato

A fool sees not the same tree that a wise man sees. William Blake

William Blake

I owe everything to a system that made me learn by heart till I wept. As a result I have thousands of lines of poetry by heart. I owe everything to this.

George Steiner

Today, more than ever before, life must be characterised by a sense of universal responsibility, not only nation to nation and human to human, but also human to other forms of life. Dalai Lama

Dalai Lama

Philosophy is like trying to open a safe with a combination lock: each little adjustment of the dials seems to achieve nothing, only when everything is in place does the door open. Ludwig Wittgenstein

And those whose hearts are fixed on reality itself deserve the title of philosophers.

Plato

The price of success in philosophy is triviality.   Clark Glymour

That Xanthippe's husband should have become so great a philosopher is remarkable. Amid all the scolding, to be able to think! But he could not write: that was impossible. Socrates has not left us a single book.   Heinrich Heine

Wonder is the feeling of a philosopher, and philosophy begins in wonder.
                                                        Socrates [quoting Plato]

Sometimes it's to your advantage for people to think you're crazy.
                                                            Thelonious Monk

Thelonious Monk

Some people never go crazy. What truly horrible lives they must live.
                                                          Charles Bukowski

Charles Bukowski

Prayer doesn't change God, but changes him who prays.   Søren Kierkegaard

Be that self which one truly is.   Søren Kierkegaard

Søren Kierkegaard

If you have knowledge, let others light their candles at it.   Margaret Fuller

The third big war will begin when the big city is burning.   Nostradamus

Nostradamus

Philosophy: A route of many roads leading from nowhere to nothing.
                                                    Ambrose Bierce

Ancient metaphysics underwent many changes at the hands of medieval thinkers who brought it in line with the dominant religious and theological movements of their day.   Wilhelm Dilthey

Metaphysics is a dark ocean without shores or lighthouse, strewn with many a philosophic wreck.   Immanuel Kant

Immanuel Kant

Language has created the word loneliness to express the pain of being alone, and the word solitude to express the glory of being alone.   Paul Tillich

Philosophers have argued for centuries about how many angels can dance on the head of a pin, but materialists have always known it depends on whether they are jitterbugging or dancing cheek to cheek.   Tom Robbins

It is easy to build a philosophy – it doesn't have to run.

Charles Franklin Kettering

I do not know how to teach philosophy without becoming a disturber of established religion.   Baruch Spinoza

Baruch Spinoza

One of my favorite philosophical tenets is that people will agree with you only if they already agree with you. You do not change people's mind.   Frank Zappa

Frank Zappa

The essence of philosophy is that a man should so live that his happiness shall depend as little as possible on external things.   Epictetus

Epictetus

A witty saying proves nothing.   Voltaire

Incomprehensibility is a far cry from deep thought.   Marcel Reich-Ranicki

This question is too good to spoil it with an answer.   Robert Koch

... After all, all he did was string together a lot of old, well-known quotations. [on Shakespeare]   Henry Louis Mencken

Actions are right in proportion as they tend to promote happiness; wrong as they tend to produce the reverse of happiness. By happiness is intended pleasure and the absence of pain.   John Stuart Mill

Do nothing, and all is done.   Lao-Tzu

A peaceful man does more good than a learned one.   Pope John XXIII

Pope John XXIII

God is really only another artist. He invented the giraffe, the elephant and the cat.
He has no real style, He just goes on trying other things.   Pablo Picasso

Pablo Picasso

No excellent soul is exempt from a mixture of madness.   Aristotle

Confessions may be good for the soul, but they are bad for the reputation.
                                                  Sir Thomas Robert Dewar

Confession is good for the soul, but bad for the career.   Peter de Vries

You can never expect a man to reveal the full truth about himself.
Marcel Reich-Ranicki

Marcel Reich-Ranicki

There are three things I always forget. Names, faces – the third I can't remember.
Italo Svevo

A myth is a religion in which no-one any longer believes.   James Feibleman

Every man takes the limits of his own field of vision for the limits of the world.
Arthur Schopenhauer

Only one man ever understood me. And he didn't understand me.
Georg Wilhelm Friedrich Hegel [complaining on his deathbed]

I often quote myself; it adds spice to my conversation.   George Bernard Shaw

Once the realisation is accepted that even between the closest human beings infinite distances continue to exist, a wonderful living side by side can grow up,
if they succeed in loving the distance between them which makes it possible for
each to see each other whole against the sky.   Rainer Maria Rilke

As we look at the stars and let our minds wander into the many galaxies, we
come to feel so small and insignificant that anything we do, say, or think seems
completely useless. But if we look into our souls and let our minds wander into
the endless galaxies of our interior lives, we become so tall and significant that
everything we do, say, or think appears of great importance.
Thomas Wright of Durham

Stretching his hand up to reach the stars, too often man forgets the flowers at his
feet.   Jeremy Bentham

Technological progress has merely provided us with more efficient means for going backwards.   Aldous Huxley

Those who educate children well are more to be honored than parents, for these
only gave life, those the art of living well.   Aristotle

Aristotle

All reality consists of a series of emanations, the eternal source of all being. The
first, necessary emanation is that of mind or intelligence, the second that of the
soul. At the periphery of the Universe is found matter. Man belongs partly in the
realm of spirit and partly in the sphere of matter.   Plotinus

The world of reality has its limits; the world of imagination is boundless.
                                                                Jean-Jacques Rousseau

Jean-Jacques Rousseau

One of Crete's own prophets has said it: 'Cretans are always liars, evil brutes, lazy
gluttons'.   Epimenides

This is the precept by which I have lived: Prepare for the worst; expect the best;
and take what comes.   Hannah Arendt

Nothing can be more real, or concern us more, than our own sentiments of pleasure and uneasiness; and if these be favourable to virtue and unfavourable to vice, no more can be requisite to the regulation of our conduct and behavior.

David Hume

David Hume

The sad truth is that most evil is done by people who never make up their minds to be either good or evil.   Hannah Arendt

Hannah Arendt

Anybody can do bad work, but not everybody does good work.   Paul Simon

Ill deeds are doubled with an evil word.   William Shakespeare

Evil deeds do not prosper; the slow man catches up with the swift.   Homer

Homer

Sometimes the old structures must be pulled down so enable the development of new ideas and to create a new order and harmony.   Peter Joseph Lenné

Peter Joseph Lenné

Man with all his shrewdness is as stupid about understanding by himself the mysteries of God, as an ass is incapable of understanding musical harmony.
John Calvin

Chapter 4

Psychology Quotes

4.1 Reason

Most of the evils of life arise from man's being unable to sit still in a room.

Blaise Pascal

Blaise Pascal

Nothing is ever accomplished by a reasonable man. Bucy's Law

The surest protection against temptation is cowardice. Mark Twain

Good people do not need laws to tell them to act responsibly, while bad people will find a way around the laws. Plato

In matters of conscience, the law of the majority has no place.

Mahatma Gandhi

He who stops being better stops being good. Oliver Cromwell

Men are like wine – some turn to vinegar, but the best improve with age.

Pope John XXIII

Freedom of conscience entails more dangers than authority and despotism.

Michel Foucault

The only tyrant I accept in this world is the still voice within.

Mahatma Gandhi

It is not only what we do, but also what we do not do, for which we are accountable.   Molière

Molière

From a moral point of view, there is no excuse for terrorist acts, regardless of the motive or the situation under which they are carried out.   Jürgen Habermas

I have only one true and real enemy in the world, and that is me.

Christian Morgenstern

One never really knows who one's enemy is.

Jürgen Habermas

Jürgen Habermas

Superstition is to religion what astrology is to astronomy: the mad daughter of a wise mother.

Voltaire

Voltaire

Religion is something left over from the infancy of our intelligence; it will fade away as we adopt reason and science as our guidelines.

Bertrand A. W. Russell

It was the experience of mystery – even if mixed with fear – that engendered religion.

Albert Einstein

Everything great in the world comes from neurotics. They alone have founded our religions and composed our masterpieces.

Marcel Proust

I prefer rationalism to atheism. The question of God and other objects-of-faith are outside reason and play no part in rationalism, thus you don't have to waste your time in either attacking or defending.   Isaac Asimov

I have a great love and respect for religion, great love and respect for atheism. What I hate is agnosticism, people who do not choose.   Orson Welles

Orson Welles

A young man who wishes to remain a sound atheist cannot be too careful of his reading.   Clive Staples Lewis

It is the humans which created God, not the other way around.

                    Ayaan Hirsi Ali

It is extremely hard for a Christian to look straight at his religion without regarding science out of the corner of his eye, or to face science without a similar side-glance at religion.   George Tyrell

I do not feel obliged to believe that the same God who has endowed us with sense, reason, and intellect has intended us to forgo their use.   Galileo Galilei

I still say a church steeple with a lightening rod on top shows a lack of confidence.
                    Doug McLeod

Wisdom is the power that enables us to use knowledge for the benefit of ourselves and others.   Thomas J. Watson

I'm a very passionate believer in the unity of knowledge. There is one world of reality – one world of our experience that we're seeking to describe.
                    John Polkinghorne

An ounce of action is worth a ton of theory.   Friedrich Engels

Friedrich Engels

If you see a formula in the Physical Review that extends over a quarter of a page, forget it. It's wrong. Nature isn't that complicated.   Bernd T. Matthias

Natural science is one of man's weapons in his fight for freedom. For the purpose of attaining freedom in society, man must use social science to understand and change society and carry out social revolution. For the purpose of attaining freedom in the world of nature, man must use natural science to understand, conquer and change nature and thus attain freedom from nature.   Mao Tse Tung

Mao Tse Tung

The hard sciences are dealing with soft problems, the soft sciences are dealing with hard problems.   Heinz von Foerster

It would be strange if the most exact of all the sciences [i.e. mathematics] had to seek support from psychology, which is still feeling its way none too surely.

Friedrich Ludwig Gottlob Frege

Friedrich Ludwig Gottlob Frege

There's nothing that can help you understand your own beliefs more than trying to explain them to an inquisitive child.   Frank Clark

If you want to see what children can do, you must stop giving them things.

Norman Douglas

What a distressing contrast there is between the radiant intelligence of the child and the feeble mentality of the average adult.   Sigmund Freud

The real magic wand is the child's own mind.   José Ortega y Gasset

José Ortega y Gasset

A child becomes an adult when he realises that he has a right not only to be right but also to be wrong.   Thomas S. Szasz

The object of teaching a child is to enable him to get along without a teacher.

Elbert Green Hubbard

Education is the best provision for old age.   Aristotle

Education is what remains after one has forgotten what one has learned in school.

Albert Einstein

Human beings, who are almost unique in having the ability to learn from the experience of others, are also remarkable for their apparent disinclination to do so.   Douglas Adams

It is better to be guided by ones experiences rather than by ones intentions and aims.   Martin Walser

Martin Walser

Experience is directly proportional to the amount of equipment ruined.

Virgil Thomson

Truth is what stands the test of experience.   Albert Einstein

You must accept the truth from whatever source it comes.

Maimonides (Moshe Ben Maimon)

Facts are many, but the truth is one.   Rabindranath Tagore

It is an old maxim of mine that when you have excluded the impossible, whatever remains, however improbable, must be the truth.   Sir Arthur Conan Doyle

The truth has never been of any real value to any human being – it is a symbol for mathematicians and philosophers to pursue. In human relations kindness and lies are worth a thousand truths.   Graham Greene

Advertisements contain the only truths to be relied on in a newspaper.

Thomas Jefferson

Thomas Jefferson

Falsehood is easy, truth so difficult.   George Eliot

Advertising is legalised lying.   Herbert George Wells

Herbert George Wells

Lying is done with words and also with silence.   Adrienne Rich

Always tell the truth. That way, you don't have to remember what you said.

Marc Twain

He who is not sure of his memory should not undertake the trade of lying.

Michel Eyquem Montaigne

The first principle is that you must not fool yourself – and you are the easiest person to fool.   Richard P. Feynman

You can fool some of the people all of the time, and all of the people some of the time, but you can not fool all of the people all of the time.   Abraham Lincoln

People never notice anything.   Jerome D. Salinger

Teach thy tongue to say 'I do not know,' and thou shalt progress.
                                         Maimonides (Moshe Ben Maimon)

Maimonides (Moshe Ben Maimon)

Better to remain silent and be thought a fool than to speak out and remove all doubt.   Abraham Lincoln

Abraham Lincoln

Rest satisfied with doing well, and leave others to talk of you as they please.
                                                                  Pythagoras

Take a rest; a field that has rested gives a beautiful crop.   Ovid

Be slow in considering, but resolute in action.   Bias of Priene

Bias of Priene

Reason is immortal, all else mortal.   Pythagoras

Thinking begins only when we have come to know that reason, glorified for centuries, is the stiff-necked adversary of thought.   Martin Heidegger

Follow where reason leads.   Zeno of Citium

Zeno of Citium

A man has free choice to the extent that he is rational.   St. Thomas Aquinas

I would not think that philosophy and reason themselves will be man's guide in the foreseeable future; however, they will remain the most beautiful sanctuary they have always been for the select few.   Albert Einstein

Reason in man is rather like God in the world.   St. Thomas Aquinas

Reason is God's crowning gift to man.   Sophocles

Sophocles

The fact that a believer is happier than a skeptic is no more to the point than the fact that a drunken man is happier than a sober one. The happiness of credulity is a cheap and dangerous quality.   George Bernard Shaw

The reasonable man adapts himself to the world; the unreasonable one persists in trying to adapt the world to himself. Therefore all progress depends on the unreasonable man.   George Bernard Shaw

Man is the most intelligent of the animals – and the most silly.   Diogenes

I believe one can say that sex eats up two thirds of our possible intellectuality.
                                                          Christian Morgenstern

Christian Morgenstern

Man is a rational animal who always loses his temper when called upon to act in accordance with the dictates of reason.   Orson Welles

The man who kills the animals today is the man who kills the people who get in
his way tomorrow.   Dian Fossey

I have found the missing link between the higher ape and civilized man: It is we.
                                                             Konrad Lorenz

It is as it is, and it is dreadful.   Hans Henny Jahnn

Hans Henny Jahnn

In the long run the pessimist may be right, but the optimist has a better time on
the trip.   Daniel L. Reardon

Enjoyment is not a goal; it is a feeling that accompanies important ongoing activity.   Paul Goodman

For Pleasure, Delight, Peace and Felicity live in method and temperance.
                                                        Margaret Cavendish

Success is getting what you want. Happiness is liking what you get.
                                                          H. Jackson Brown

If only we'd stop trying to be happy we could have a pretty good time.
                                                             Edith Wharton

Happiness ... it lies in the joy of achievement, in the thrill of creative effort.
                                                           Vincent van Gogh

Nothing is so good as it seems beforehand.   George Eliot

We don't see things as they are, we see them as we are.   Talmud

Look! Don't be deceived by appearances – men and things are not what they seem. All who are not on the rock are in the sea! William Booth

William Booth

Television has done much for psychiatry by spreading information about it, as well as contributing to the need for it. Alfred Hitchcock

Psychoanalysis is the mental illness it purports to cure. Karl Kraus

Karl Kraus

I don't go for this auto-cannibalism. Very damaging. [On psychoanalysis]
Peter O'Toole

In psychoanalysis, only the fee is exactly what it seems to be. Mason Cooley

Psychiatry enables us to correct our faults by confessing our parents shortcomings.
Laurence J. Peter

It had become clear to me, in a flash of illumination, that for me the only possible goal was psychiatry. Here alone the two currents of my interest could flow together and in a united stream dig their own bed. Here was the empirical field common to biological and spiritual facts, which I had everywhere sought and nowhere found. Here at last was the place where the collision of nature and spirit became a reality.   Carl Gustav Jung

Psychology which explains everything explains nothing, and we are still in doubt.
                                                         Marianne Craig Moore

Psychology has a long past, but only a short history.   Hermann Ebbinghaus

[Medicine is] a collection of uncertain prescriptions the results of which, taken collectively, are more fatal than useful to mankind.   Napoleon Bonaparte

Napoleon Bonaparte

A medical maxim – when you hear hoofbeats, think of horses before zebras.
                                                              Harley Smith

One of the first duties of the physician is to educate the masses not to take medicine.
                                                          Sir William Osler

He who joyfully marches to music in rank and file has already earned my contempt. He has been given a large brain by mistake, since for him the spinal cord would suffice.   Albert Einstein

Work cure is the best of all psychotherapy, in my opinion. ... As well might we expect a patient to recover without food as to recover without work. ... The sound man needs work to keep him sound, but the nervous invalid has an even greater need of work to draw him out of his isolation, and to stop the miseries of doubt and self-scrutiny, to win back self-respect and the support of fellowship.
                                                          Richard C. Cabot

A vigorous five-mile walk will do more good for an unhappy but otherwise healthy adult than all the medicine and psychology in the world.   Paul Dudley White

Office jobs are physically easier, but the worker takes home worries instead of an aching back.   Homer Bigart

Friendship is like an earthenware, once broken it can be mended; love is like a mirror, once broken, that ends it.   Josh Billings

Love is an ideal thing, marriage is a real thing; a confusion of the real with the ideal never goes unpunished.   Johann Wolfgang von Goethe

Marriage is the grave or tomb of wit.   Margaret Cavendish

Women, can't live with them, can't live without them.   Erasmus of Rotterdam

There's enough uncertainty about marriage without sitting home wondering what tree your husband is hanging from that night.   Lola Montez

Lola Montez

Do not rely completely on any other human being. We meet all life's greatest tests alone.   Agnes MacPhail

We're born alone, we live alone, we die alone. Only through our love and friendship can we create the illusion for the moment that we're not alone.
                                                                          Orson Welles

If you are afraid of being lonely, don't try to be right.   Jules Renard

There are no such things as conversation. It is an illusion. There are intersecting monologues, that is all.   Rebecca West

Rebecca West

By increasing the size of the keyhole, today's playwrights are in danger of doing away with the door.   Peter Ustinov

Peter Ustinov

I hate crowds and making speeches. I hate facing cameras and having to answer to a crossfire of questions. Why popular fancy should seize upon me, a scientist, dealing in abstract things and happy if left alone, is a manifestation of mass psychology that is beyond me.   Albert Einstein

Although a skillful flatterer is a most delightful companion if you have him all to yourself, his taste becomes very doubtful when he takes to complimenting other people.   Charles Dickens

The nice thing about being a celebrity is that when you bore people, they think it's their fault.   Henry Kissinger

Be courteous to all, but intimate with few; and let those few be well tried before you give them your confidence.   George Washington

George Washington

Half a psychiatrist's patients see him because they are married – the other half because they're not.   Arnold H. Glasgow

A psychiatrist is a man who goes to the Folies-Bergère and looks at the audience.
                                                                    Bishop Mervyn Stockwood

Show me a sane man and I will cure him for you.   Carl Gustav Jung

Psychiatric expert testimony: mendacity masquerading as medicine.
                                                                          Thomas S. Szasz

Thomas S. Szasz

Psychoanalysis is not a science [and it is] perhaps more like witch-doctoring.

Richard P. Feynman

Psychoanalysis is confession without absolution.   Gilbert Keith Chesterton

But psychoanalysis has taught that the dead – a dead parent, for example – can be more alive for us, more powerful, more scary, than the living. It is the question of ghosts.   Jacques Derrida

Jacques Derrida

Psychologists think they're experimental psychologists.
Experimental psychologists think they're biologists.
Biologists think they're biochemists.
Biochemists think they're chemists.
Chemists think they're physical chemists.
Physical chemists think they're physicists.
Physicists think they're theoretical physicists.
Theoretical physicists think they're mathematicians.
Mathematicians think they're metamathematicians.
Metamathematicians think they're philosophers.
Philosophers think they're gods.   Anonymous

Psychiatry is probably the single most destructive force that has affected the American society within the last fifty years.   Thomas S. Szasz

Psychiatry lies somewhere between astrology and phrenology on the scale of human gullibility.   Gore Vidal

Psychology keeps trying to vindicate human nature. History keeps undermining the effort.   Mason Cooley

No human being can really understand another, and no one can arrange another's happiness.   Graham Greene

The science of the mind can only have for its proper goal the understanding of human nature by every human being, and through its use, brings peace to every human soul.   Alfred Adler

I've come to the conclusion that it's not really possible to help others.
                                                       Paul Cezanne

Paul Cezanne

You can put anything into words, except your own life.   Max Frisch

You ask me why I do not write something ... I think one's feelings waste themselves in words, they ought all to be distilled into actions and into actions which bring results.   Florence Nightingale

Florence Nightingale

Writing is a form of therapy; sometimes I wonder how all those, who do not write, compose, or paint can manage to escape the madness, the melancholia, the panic fear, which is inherent in a human condition.   Graham Greene

Words are all we have.   Samuel Beckett

Samuel Beckett

He is a sane man who can have tragedy in his heart and comedy in his head.
                                                    Gilbert Keith Chesterton

Art is a jealous mistress, and if a man has a genius for painting, poetry, music, architecture, or philosophy, he makes a bad husband and an ill provider.
                                                      Ralph Waldo Emerson

Good breeding consists in concealing how much we think of ourselves and how little we think of the other person.   Mark Twain

So-called Christian psychology is secular psychology clothed in pious platitudes and religious rhetoric.   J. Vernon McGee

Freudianism is much more nearly a religion than a science, inasmuch as the relation between analyst and patient has a great deal in common with that between priest and communicant at confessional, and such ideas as the Oedipus complex, the superego, the libido, and the id exert an effect upon the converted which is almost identical with what flows to the devout Christian from godhead, trinity, grace, and immortality.   Robert Nisbet

An experiment at the All-India Institute of Mental Health in Bangalore found that Western-trained psychiatrists and native healers had a comparable recovery rate. The most notable difference was that the so-called "witch doctors" released their patients sooner.   American Psychiatric Association

To mature means to take responsibility for your life, to be on your own. Psycho-analysis fosters the infantile state by considering that the past is responsible for the illness.   Fritz Perls

Three-quarters of the sicknesses of intelligent people come from their intelligence. They need at least a doctor who can understand this sickness.   Marcel Proust

Most of the vices and mortal sins condemned today correspond to inclinations that were purely adaptive or at least harmless in primitive man.   Konrad Lorenz

Konrad Lorenz

Most people believe that sin is an offense against the diet sheet.

Eugen Drewermann

Eugen Drewermann

Marx, Darwin and Freud are the three most crashing bores of the Western World. Simplistic popularisation of their ideas has thrust our world into a mental strait-jacket from which we can only escape by the most anarchic violence.

William Golding

The first human who hurled an insult instead of a stone was the founder of civilization.

Sigmund Freud

One machine can do the work of fifty ordinary men. No machine can do the work of one extraordinary man.

Elbert Green Hubbard

Above all, however, the machine has no feelings, it feels no fear and no hope ... it operates according to the pure logic of probability. For this reason I assert that the robot perceives more accurately than man.

Max Frisch

Max Frisch

Soon silence will have passed into legend. Man has turned his back on silence. Day after day he invents machines and devices that increase noise and distract humanity from the essence of life, contemplation, meditation.

Hans Arp

Hans Arp

It is easy to give advice from a port of safety.   Friedrich Schiller

One-half of life is luck; the other half is discipline – and that's the important half, for without discipline you wouldn't know what to do with luck.

Carl Zuckmayer

Carl Zuckmayer

The belief that one's own view of reality is the only reality is the most dangerous of all delusions.   Paul Watzlawick

Paul Watzlawick

Anyone who cannot come to terms with his life while he is alive needs one hand to ward off a little his despair over his fate ... but with his other hand he can note down what he sees among the ruins.   Franz Kafka

Not a shred of evidence exists in favour of the idea that life is serious.

Brendan Gill

It's precisely the disappointing stories, which have no proper ending and therefore no proper meaning, that sound true to life.   Max Frisch

Reality is a question of perspective; the further you get from the past, the more concrete and plausible it seems – but as you approach the present, it inevitably seems incredible.   Salman Rushdie

He who confronts the paradoxical exposes himself to reality.
                                                                Friedrich Dürrenmatt

Friedrich Dürrenmatt

Why do we pay for psychotherapy when massages cost half as much?
                                                                Jason Love

A neurotic is a man who builds a castle in the air. A psychotic is the man who lives in it. A psychiatrist is the man who collects the rent.   Jerome Lawrence

A mistake which is commonly made about neurotics is to suppose that they are interesting. It is not interesting to be always unhappy, engrossed with oneself, malignant and ungrateful, and never quite in touch with reality.
                                                                Cyril Connolly

I envy paranoids; they actually feel people are paying attention to them.
                                                                Susan Sontag

Men will always be mad, and those who think they can cure them are the maddest of all.   Voltaire

Madness need not be all breakdown. It may also be break-through.
                                                                Ronald David Laing

Every form of addiction is bad, no matter whether the narcotic be alcohol, morphine or idealism. Carl Gustav Jung

Carl Gustav Jung

Everything that irritates us about others can lead us to a better understanding of ourselves. Carl Gustav Jung

He who knows much about others may be learned, but he who understands himself is more intelligent. He who controls others may be powerful, but he who has mastered himself is mightier still. Lao-Tzu

How awful to reflect that what people say of us is true. Logan Pearsall Smith

In general, certain conclusions are possible from these data. They fail to prove that psychotherapy, Freudian or otherwise, facilitates the recovery of neurotic patients. Hans Eysenck

A neurosis is a secret you don't know you are keeping. Kenneth Tynan

Neurosis is no worse than a bad cold; you ache all over, and it's made you a mess, but you won't die from it. Mignon McLaughlin

Computers can't simulate truly human behavior yet, but then neither can most people. Dean Hannotte

Electric communication will never be a substitute for the face of someone who with their soul encourages another person to be brave and true. Charles Dickens

Handwriting is autobiography. Carrie Latet

Human affairs are so obscure and various that nothing can be clearly known.

Erasmus of Rotterdam

It always seemed strange to me that the things we admire in men, kindness and generosity, openness, honesty, understanding and feeling are the concomitants of failure in our system. And those traits we detest, sharpness, greed, acquisitiveness, meanness, egotism and selfinterest are the traits of success. And while men admire the quality of the first, they love the produce of the second.   John Steinbeck

John Steinbeck

While the individual man is an insoluble puzzle, in the aggregate he becomes a mathematical certainty.

Sherlock Holmes, the fictional creation of Sir Arthur Conan Doyle

An audience is never wrong. An individual member of it may be an imbecile, but a thousand imbeciles together in the dark – that is critical genius.   Billy Wilder

A wonderful fact to reflect upon, that every human creature is constituted to be that profound secret and mystery to every other.   Charles Dickens

Charles Dickens

Noble deeds and hot baths are the best cures for depression.   Dodie Smith

Anyone who hates dogs and kids can't be all bad.   William Claude Fields

Extraordinary claims demand extraordinary proof. There are many examples of outsiders who eventually overthrew entrenched scientific orthodoxies, but they prevailed with irrefutable data. More often, egregious findings that contradict well-established research turn out to be artifacts. I have argued that accepting psychic powers, reincarnation, "cosmic consciousness," and the like, would entail fundamental revisions of the foundations of neuroscience. Before abandoning materialist theories of mind that have paid handsome dividends, we should insist on better evidence for psi phenomena than presently exists, especially when neurology and psychology themselves offer more plausible alternatives.

Barry L. Beyerstein

When the mind is thinking it is talking to itself.   Plato

What is mind? No matter. What is matter? Never mind.   George Berkeley

George Berkeley

To be too conscious is an illness – a real thoroughgoing illness.

Fyodor Dostoevsky

What if everything is an illusion and nothing exists? In that case, I definitely overpaid for my carpet.   Woody Allen [Without Feathers]

Hypochondria is Greek for men.   Kathy Lette

It is the genus that gives the characters, and not the characters that make the genus.

Carl Linnaeus

Your soul is a dark forest. But the trees are of a particular species, they are ge-
nealogical trees.   Marcel Proust

In Nature, we have as clear an understanding as men, if we were bred in Schools
to Mature our Brains.   Margaret Cavendish

Margaret Cavendish

I know that it is a good move, but I don't know why it is a good move.
                                                        José Raúl Capablanca

4.2 Courage

If a lot of cures are suggested for a disease, it means that the disease is incurable.
                                                                Anton Chekhov

Diseases are the tax on pleasures.   John Ray

Boredom is the root of all evil – the despairing refusal to be oneself.
                                                            Søren Kierkegaard

Søren Kierkegaard

I have ten commandments. The first nine are, thou shalt not bore. The tenth is,
thou shalt have right of final cut.   Billy Wilder

Billy Wilder

A credit card is an anaesthetic which simply delays the pain.   Helen Mason

Do not say a little in many words but a great deal in a few.   Pythagoras

God became man, granted. The devil became a woman.   Victor Hugo

I am glad that I am not a man, as I should be obliged to marry a woman.

Madame de Staël

A woman must have money and a room of her own.   Virginia Woolf

Feminine meekness serves the cause of power in general.

Eleanor of Aquitaine

Eleanor of Aquitaine

Very learned women are to be found, in the same manner as female warriors; but they are seldom or ever inventors.   Voltaire

To be successful, a woman has to be much better at her job than a man.

Golda Meir

Golda Meir

Were there no women, man might live as gods.   Thomas Dekker

A man is as good as he has to be, and a woman as bad as she dares.
                                                               Elbert Hubbard Green

All the reasonings of men are not worth one sentiment of women.   Voltaire

Woman is the dominant sex. Men have to do all sorts of stuff to prove that they
are worthy of woman's attention.   Camille Paglia

Children and lunatics cut the Gordian knot which the poet spends his life patiently
trying to untie.   Jean Cocteau

Man seeks to escape himself in myth, and does so by any means at his disposal.
Drugs, alcohol, or lies. Unable to withdraw into himself, he disguises himself.
Lies and inaccuracy give him a few moments of comfort.   Jean Cocteau

A good portion of speaking will consist in knowing how to lie.
                                                            Erasmus of Rotterdam

I feel more comfortable with gorillas than people. I can anticipate what a gorilla's
going to do, and they're purely motivated.   Dian Fossey

The more I see of men the more I like dogs.   Madame de Staël

Dogs are better than human beings because they know but do not tell.
                                                               Emily Dickinson

Emily Dickinson

Big results require big ambitions.   Heraclitus of Ephesus

In great attempts it is glorious even to fail.   Cassius

Security is a kind of death.   Tennessee Williams

Man is ready to die for an idea, provided that idea is not quite clear to him.
                    Paul Eldridge

Here I stand; I can do no other. God help me. Amen!   Martin Luther

Martin Luther

A heretic is a man who sees with his own eyes.   Gotthold Ephraim Lessing

Heresy is another word for freedom of thought.   Graham Greene

There is nothing more wonderful than freedom of speech.   Ilya Ehrenburg

God is rubbish. Life is the main thing.   Arnold Zweig

You can't base your life on other people's expectations.   Stevie Wonder

Stevie Wonder

Always be a first-rate version of yourself, instead of a second-rate version of somebody else.   Judy Garland

I have the true feeling of myself only when I am unbearably unhappy.
                                                                              Franz Kafka

I am a kind of paranoiac in reverse. I suspect people of plotting to make me happy.
                                                                         Jerome D. Salinger

Jerome D. Salinger

Laziness belongs to the most exquisite enjoyments of human life. But like all delicatessen, laziness should only be consumed in small quantities. Laziness has to melt in ones mouth with pleasure. In excess, it tastes disgusting, and if laziness is forced upon you, it even creates pain.   Heinrich Spoerl

Heinrich Spoerl

Idleness is the parent of psychology.   Friedrich Nietzsche

The most important thing to do in your life, is to not interfere with somebody else's life.   Frank Zappa

Anyone who goes to a psychiatrist ought to have his head examined.

Samuel Goldwyn

Samuel Goldwyn

When people do not respect us we are sharply offended; yet deep down in his heart no man much respects himself.   Marc Twain

A sound mind in a sound body is a short but full description of a happy state in this world.   John Locke

Have no fear of perfection – you'll never reach it.   Salvador Dalí

Salvador Dalí

I expected more from literature than from real, naked life.   Günter Grass

Music is the mediator between the spiritual and the sensual life.

Ludwig van Beethoven

Dance with all the might of your body, and all the fire of your soul, in order that you may shake all melancholy out of your liver.   Lola Montez

True friendship is like sound health; the value of it is seldom known until it is lost.   Charles Colton

Everyone wants to have a friend, but nobody takes the trouble to be one.
Alfred Kerr

Alfred Kerr

I argue very well. Ask any of my remaining friends. I can win an argument on any topic, against any opponent. People know this, and steer clear of me at parties. Often, as a sign of their great respect, they don't even invite me.   Dave Barry

Sleep, riches, and health, to be truly enjoyed must be interrupted.
Jean Paul Richter

Attention to health is life's greatest hindrance.   Plato

Nothing is so wonderful when you get used to it.   Edgar Watson Howe

How many women does one need to sing the scale of love all the way up and down?   Georg Büchner

Georg Büchner

We are only puppets, our strings are being pulled by unknown forces.

Georg Büchner

Love is a peculiar thing.

Georg Büchner

You yourself, as much as anybody in the entire universe, deserve your love and affection.   Buddha

After the verb "to love," "to help" is the most beautiful verb in the world.

Bertha von Suttner

Bertha von Suttner

Nothing makes one feel so strong as a call for help.   Pope Paul VI

Kindness is a language which the deaf can hear and the blind can read.

Mark Twain

Every time you smile at someone, it is an action of love, a gift to that person, a beautiful thing.   Mother Teresa

Though we travel the world over to find the beautiful, we must carry it with us, or we find it not.   Ralph Waldo Emerson

Life has got a habit of not standing hitched. You got to ride it like you find it. You got to change with it. If a day goes by that don't change some of your old notions for new ones, that is just about like trying to milk a dead cow.   Woody Guthrie

Nothing is easier than to break a taboo, and nothing is more difficult to live peacefully together.   Alexander Mitscherlich

Be peaceful, be courteous, obey the law, respect everyone; but if someone puts his hand on you, send him to the cemetery.   Malcolm X

You cannot find peace by avoiding life.   Virginia Woolf

Tact is the ability to describe others as they see themselves.   Abraham Lincoln

The aim of psychoanalysis is to relieve people of their neurotic unhappiness so
that they can be normally unhappy.   Sigmund Freud

Sigmund Freud

Nothing is funnier than unhappiness, I grant you that. Yes, yes, it's the most
comical thing in the world.   Samuel Beckett

Neurosis is always a substitute for legitimate suffering.   Carl Gustav Jung

I was seized by the stern hand of compulsion, that dark, unseasonable Urge that
impels women to clean house in the middle of the night.   James Thurber

James Thurber

An actual stroll through a lunatic asylum shows that faith does not prove anything.
Friedrich Nietzsche

It might be said of psychoanalysis that if you give it your little finger it will soon have your whole hand.   Sigmund Freud

It is your work in life that is the ultimate seduction.   Pablo Picasso

One of the symptoms of an approaching nervous breakdown is the belief that one's work is terribly important.   Bertrand A. W. Russell

If I were a medical man, I should prescribe a holiday to any patient who considers his work important.   Bertrand A. W. Russell

I don't suffer from insanity but enjoy every minute of it.   Edgar Allen Poe

I doubt if a single individual could be found from the whole of mankind free from some form of insanity. The only difference is one of degree. A man who sees a gourd and takes it for his wife is called insane because this happens to very few people.   Erasmus of Rotterdam

Life is really simple, but we insist on making it complicated.   Confucius

Confucius

A psychiatrist is a fellow who asks you a lot of expensive questions your wife asks for nothing.   Joey Adams

One should only see a psychiatrist out of boredom.   Muriel Spark

The personal history is never like uniformly running water, since it will for sure be stopped occasionally by a dam and thus go in circles, or that people will throw stones into the clear water.   Fritz Reuter

Fritz Reuter

Never forget that only dead fish swim with the stream.   Malcolm Muggeridge

Life is a series of crises separated by brief periods of self-delusion.
                                                                    Richard Rosen

You are here only for a short visit. Don't hurry, don't worry. And be sure to smell the flowers along the way.   Walter Hagen

Laughter is the tonic, the relief, the surcease for pain.   Charlie Chaplin

Charlie Chaplin

Always laugh when you can. It is cheap medicine.   Lord Byron

The human race has one really effective weapon, and that is laughter.
                                                                        Mark Twain

Many people believe that they are attracted by God, or by Nature, when they are
only repelled by man.   William Ralph Inge

The closer you get to know important people, the more disagreeable they get.
                                                            Marcel Reich-Ranicki

Living is a disease from which sleep gives us relief eight hours a day.
                                              Sebastien-Roch Nicolas de Chamfort

Sebastien-Roch Nicolas de Chamfort

A person is a success if they get up in the morning and gets to bed at night and in
between does what he wants to do.   Bob Dylan

Blessed is the person who is too busy to worry in the daytime, and too sleepy to
worry at night.   Leo Aikman

One of the characteristics of the dream is that nothing surprises us in it. With no
regret, we agree to live in it with strangers, completely cut off from our habits and
friends.   Jean Cocteau

There are some people who live in a dream world, and there are some who face
reality; and then there are those who turn one into the other.
                                                            Erasmus of Rotterdam

It is far harder to kill a phantom than a reality.   Virginia Woolf

Imagination creates reality.   Richard Wagner

Richard Wagner

Life is perhaps most widely regarded as a bad dream between two awakenings and every day is a life in miniature.   Eugene O'Neill

Eugene O'Neill

I can't go on. I'll go on.   Samuel Beckett

We are all born mad. Some remain so.   Samuel Beckett

We start off confused and end up confused on higher level.   Alan Chalmers

The cat, having sat upon a hot stove lid, will not sit upon a hot stove lid again. Nor on a cold stove lid.   Marc Twain

The purpose of psychology is to give us a completely different idea of the things we know best.   Paul Valéry

Complete abstinence is easier than perfect moderation.   St. Augustine

There are times when parenthood seems nothing but feeding the mouth that bites you.   Peter de Vries

It is easy to become a father, but very difficult to be a father.   Wilhelm Busch

We are always too busy for our children; we never give them the time or interest they deserve. We lavish gifts upon them; but the most precious gift – our personal association, which means so much to them – we give grudgingly.   Mark Twain

Being born is like being kidnapped. And then sold into slavery.   Andy Warhol

Andy Warhol

Insanity is hereditary. You can get it from your children.   Sam Levenson

It must be a hard life to be the child of a psychologist.   Tom Masson

We don't inherit the Earth from our ancestors, we borrow it from our children.
                                    David R. Brower

She generally gave herself very good advice, (though she very seldom followed it).   Lewis Carroll

Time spent with cats is never wasted. Sigmund Freud

Man is the only animal for whom his own existence is a problem which he has to solve. Erich Fromm

There is no psychology; there is only biography and autobiography.
Thomas S. Szasz

A wise man should not strive to eliminate his complexes but to get into accord with them: they are legitimately what directs his conduct in the world.
Sigmund Freud

If you talk to God, you are praying. If God talks to you, you have schizophrenia.
Thomas S. Szasz

If you can play as if it means nothing when it means everything, then you are hard to beat. Steve Davis

The mass of men lead lives of quiet desperation. Henry D. Thoreau

Ordinarily he was insane, but he had lucid moments when he was merely stupid.
Heinrich Heine

Heinrich Heine

The field of psychology today is literally a mess. There are as many techniques, methods, and theories around as there are researchers and therapists. I have personally seen therapists convince their clients that all of their problems come from their mothers, the stars, their bio-chemical makeup, their diet, their lifestyle, and even the "kharma" from their past lives. Roger Mills

I myself spent nine years in an insane asylum and I never had the obsession of suicide, but I know that each conversation with a psychiatrist, every morning at the time of his visit, made me want to hang myself, realising that I would not be able to cut his throat.   Antonin Artaud

The law, in its majestic equality, forbids the rich as well as the poor to sleep under bridges, to beg in the streets and steal bread.   Anatole France

Each morning I shoo the beggars and cripples from my door stoop. If God wanted these vermin to eat surely he would provide them with substance.

Peter Paul Rubens

Peter Paul Rubens

If a man devotes himself to art, much evil is avoided that happens otherwise if one is idle.   Albrecht Dürer

Albrecht Dürer

Formerly, when religion was strong and science weak, men mistook magic for medicine; now, when science is strong and religion weak, men mistake medicine for magic.   Thomas S. Szasz

To study the abnormal is the best way of understanding the normal.

William James

Let us a little permit Nature to take her own way; she better understands her own affairs than we.   Michel Eyquen Montaigne

No psychologist should pretend to understand what he does not understand. Only fools and charlatans know everything and understand nothing.

Anton Chekhov

If my devils are to leave me, I am afraid my angels will take flight as well.

Rainer Maria Rilke

I can't explain myself, I'm afraid, because I'm not myself, you see.

Lewis Carroll

We only really face up to ourselves when we are afraid.   Thomas Bernhard

Thomas Bernhard

Horror is beyond the reach of psychology.   Theodor W. Adorno

A psychiatrist is the next man you will start talking to after you have started talking to yourself.   Wystan Hugh Auden

I do think psychiatry is a waste of good couches. Why should I make a psychiatrist laugh, and then pay him?   Kathy Lette

Psychiatry is the art of teaching people how to stand on their own two feet while reclining on couches.   Sigmund Freud

If the nineteenth century was the age of the editorial chair, ours is the century of
the psychiatrist's couch.   Marshall McLuhan

Psychoanalysis is not the only way to resolve inner conflicts. Life itself still remains a very effective therapist.   Karen Horney

There are cases where psychoanalysis works worse than anything else. But who
said that psychoanalysis was to be applied always and everywhere.

Carl Gustav Jung

There are now electrical appliances with the main unit so sealed in that it cannot
be got at for repair. There have always been human beings like that.

Mignon McLaughlin

Depressed people think they know themselves, but maybe they only know depression.   Mark Epstein

A wonderful discovery, psychoanalysis. Makes quite simple people feel they're
complex.   Samuel N. Behrman

Freud is the father of psychoanalysis. It had no mother.   Germaine Greer

In a time of universal deceit, telling the truth is a revolutionary act.

George Orwell

It is always the best policy to tell the truth, provided of course you happen to be
an exceptionally good liar.   Jerome K. Jerome

Great souls suffer in silence.   Friedrich Schiller

You must submit to supreme suffering in order to discover the completion of joy.
John Calvin

John Calvin

It is difficult to imagine how any behavior in the presence of another person can avoid being a communication of one's own view of the nature of one's relationship with that person and how it can fail to influence that person.   Paul Watzlawick

I guess the definition of a lunatic is a man surrounded by them.   Ezra Pound

Ezra Pound

The easiest kind of relationship for me is with ten thousand people. The hardest is with one.   Joan Baez

All poetic inspiration is but dream interpretation.   Hans Sachs

Hans Sachs

In places like universities, where everyone talks too rationally, it is necessary for a kind of enchanter to appear.   Joseph Beuys

When I was in school, I cheated on my metaphysics exam: I looked into the soul of the boy sitting next to me.   Woody Allen

In a museum in Havana, there are two skulls of Christopher Columbus, "one when he was a boy and one when he was a man."   Mark Twain

Some day humans will have to fight the noise as vehemently as cholera and plague.

Robert Koch

The profession of a prostitute is the only career in which the maximum income is paid to the newest apprentice.

William Booth

Unemployment can only be fought, if the employed are ready to pass on part of their job to the unemployed, including part of their income.

Oswald von Nell-Breuning

Oswald von Nell-Breuning

In a few years we will all be socialists – either we share the few things that we have, or there will be nothing left for anybody.

Leonardo Boff

Never fear mighty men.

Eleanor of Aquitaine

A man does not have to be an angel in order to be a saint.

Albert Schweitzer

Albert Schweitzer

Anyone who seeks to destroy the passions instead of controlling them is trying to play the angel.

Voltaire

I am not a saint, unless you think of a saint as a sinner who keeps on trying.

Nelson Mandela

I know God will not give me anything I can't handle. I just wish that He didn't trust me so much.

Mother Teresa

Mother Teresa

Let no one ever come to you without leaving better and happier.

Mother Teresa

4.3   Desire

The wine urges me on, the bewitching wine, which sets even a wise man to singing and to laughing gently and rouses him up to dance and brings forth words which were better unspoken.

Homer

An alcoholic is a person who drinks more than his doctor.

Anonymous

Of course one should not drink much, but often.

Henri Toulouse-Lautrec

Henri Toulouse-Lautrec

The best magnifying glasses for the joys in the world are those from which one drinks.

Joachim Ringelnatz

Some things need to be believed to be seen.

Guy Kawasaki

By believing passionately in something that still does not exist, we create it. The nonexistent is whatever we have not sufficiently desired.

Franz Kafka

A man sees what he wants to see, and disregards the rest.

Paul Simon

Libenter homines id quod volunt credunt. (Men gladly believe that which they wish for.)

Julius Caesar

Thinking, we shape the objects of our thoughts.

Christian Morgenstern

Man prefers to believe what he prefers to be true. Francis Bacon

Francis Bacon

The actions of men are the best interpreters of their thoughts. James Joyce

Nothing is easier than self-deceit. For what each man wishes, that he also believes to be true. Demosthenes

Glory is like a circle in the water, Which never ceaseth to enlarge itself, till by broad spreading it disperses to naught. William Shakespeare

William Shakespeare

The deepest principle of human nature is the craving to be appreciated.
William James

The desire to write grows with writing. Erasmus of Rotterdam

By reading the characteristic features of any man's castles in the air you can make a shrewd guess as to his underlying desires which are frustrated.   John Dewey

I'm always thinking about creating. My future starts when I wake up every morning ... Every day I find something creative to do with my life.   Miles Davis

Miles Davis

A man must make his opportunity, as oft as find it.   Francis Bacon

Ability may get you to the top, but it takes character to keep you there.
Stevie Wonder

Music was our wife, and we loved her. And we stayed with her, and we clothed her, and we put diamond rings on her hands.   Lionel Hampton

Lionel Hampton

A lot of disappointed people have been left standing on the street corner waiting for the bus marked Perfection.   Donald Kennedy

There are only two tragedies in life: one is not getting what one wants, and the other is getting it. Oscar Wilde

There are two things to aim at in life: first, to get what you want; and after that, to enjoy it. Only the wisest of mankind achieve the second.

Logan Pearsall Smith

We crucify ourselves between two thieves; regret for yesterday and fear for to-morrow. Fulton Oursler

My friend, let's not think of tomorrow, but let's enjoy this fleeting moment of life.

Omar Al-Khayyam

Omar Al-Khayyam

It isn't where you came from, its where you're going that counts.

Ella Fitzgerald

Ella Fitzgerald

I wanted to change the world. But I have found that the only thing one can be sure
of changing is oneself.   Aldous Huxley

All forms of tampering with human beings, getting at them, shaping them against
their will to your own pattern, all thought control and conditioning is, therefore, a
denial of that in men which makes them men and their values ultimate.
                                                                              Isaiah Berlin

In politics, as on the sick bed, people toss from side to side, thinking they will be
more comfortable.   Johann Wolfgang von Goethe

Ninety percent of the politicians give the other ten percent a bad reputation.
                                                                          Henry Kissinger

A democratic government is the only one in which those who vote for a tax can
escape the obligation to pay it.   Alexis de Tocqueville

Alexis de Tocqueville

Wonder is the desire for knowledge.   St. Thomas Aquinas

No miracle has ever taken place under conditions science can accept. Experience
shows, without exception, that miracles occur only in times and in countries in
which miracles are believed in, and in the presence of persons who are disposed
to believe them.   Ernest Renan

Miracles in the sense of events contrary to the laws of nature so far from demon-
strating to us the existence of God, would on the contrary lead us to doubt it.
                                                                         Stuart Kauffman

It is the stars, the stars above us govern our conditions.   William Shakespeare

As contraries are known by contraries, so is the delight of presence best known by the torments of absence.   Alcibiades

Alcibiades

Astrology is a disease, not a science.   Maimonides (Moshe Ben Maimon)

It is not necessary that you leave the house. Remain at your table and listen. Do not even listen, only wait. Do not even wait, be wholly still and alone. The world will present itself to you for its unmasking, it can do no other, in ecstasy it will writhe at your feet.   Franz Kafka

The world would be happier if men had the same capacity to be silent that they have to speak.   Baruch Spinoza

Baruch Spinoza

If you want to cure all the world's problems, kill all the people.   Esther Dyson

Something must happen!   Heinrich Böll

Heinrich Böll

What I have seen of the love affairs of other people has not led me to regret the deficiency in my experience.   George Bernard Shaw

Perhaps people like us cannot love. Ordinary people can – that is their secret.
                                                                       Hermann Hesse

Normal love isn't interesting. I assure you that it's incredibly boring.
                                                                       Roman Polanski

Man is a clever animal who behaves like an imbecile.   Albert Schweitzer

In view of the stupidity of the majority of the people, a widely held opinion is more likely to be foolish than sensible.   Bertrand A. W. Russell

I tell you there's a monster, like all that is darkening and heavy and obstructive in life. It is matter and darkness, it is the anti-soul, it is the ruling power of this land: stupidity.   Herbert George Wells

Happiness is an illusion caused by the temporary absence of reality.
                                                                       Desmond Cleary

Happiness is nothing more than good health and a bad memory.
                                                                       Albert Schweitzer

Happiness is something that comes into our lives through doors we don't even remember leaving open.   Rose Kane

I am more and more convinced that our happiness or unhappiness depends more on the way we meet the events of life than on the nature of those events themselves. Alexander von Humboldt

Alexander von Humboldt

Let us be grateful to the people who make us happy; they are the charming gardeners who make our souls blossom. Marcel Proust

Whenever I get happy, I always have a terrible feeling. Roman Polanski

Roman Polanski

There is no fun in doing nothing when you have nothing to do. Jerome K. Jerome

Don't disturb me! I am occupied doing nothing. Claus Grupen

Let us be lazy in everything, except in loving and drinking, except in being lazy. Gotthold Ephraim Lessing

I have learned to seek my happiness by limiting my desires, rather than in attempting to satisfy them. John Stuart Mill

While living I want to live well. Sitting Bull

Sitting Bull

The discipline of desire is the background of character. John Locke

John Locke

Control thy passions, lest they take vengeance on thee. Epictetus

Give me chastity and continence, but not yet. Saint Augustine

There are no chaste minds. Minds copulate whenever they meet. Eric Heffer

I can resist anything except temptation. Oscar Wilde

God gave men both a penis and a brain, but unfortunately not enough blood supply to run both at the same time.   Robin Williams

The hypothalamus is one of the most important parts of the brain, involved in many kinds of motivation, among other functions. The hypothalamus controls the "Four F's": fighting, fleeing, feeding, and mating.   Unknown

My unconscious knows more about the consciousness of the psychologist than his consciousness knows about my unconscious.   Karl Kraus

Psychoanalysis: a rabbit that was swallowed by a boa constrictor that just wanted to see what it was like in there.   Karl Kraus

Let the credulous and the vulgar continue to believe that all mental woes can be cured by a daily application of old Greek myths to their private parts.
                                                            Vladimir Nabokov

Vladimir Nabokov

Every artist dips his brush in his own soul, and paints his own nature into his pictures.   Elisabeth Brant (Peter Paul Rubens' first wife)

Elisabeth Brant

I paint what cannot be photographed, that which comes from the imagination or from dreams, or from an unconscious drive.   Man Ray

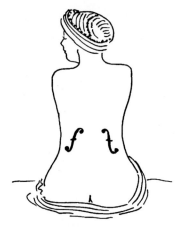

Man Ray's art

Dreams are not without meaning wherever they may come from – from fantasy, from the elements, or from other inspiration.   Paracelsus

Painting is such an incredible act, one that transcends the physical reality of what is being portrayed.   Hans Holbein the Younger

Hans Holbein the Younger

Sometimes legends make reality, and become more useful than the facts.
                                    Salman Rushdie

If I could say it in words there would be no reason to paint.   Edward Hopper

You've got to find some way of saying it without saying it.   Duke Ellington

I am seeking for the bridge which leans from the visible to the invisible through reality.   Max Beckmann

Max Beckmann

It is unfulfilled dreams that keep you alive.   Robert Schuller

The art of living is the art of bringing dreams and reality together.
                                                    Tom Hodgkinson

Dreams must be heeded and accepted. For a great many of them come true.
                                                    Paracelsus

The nicest thing for me is sleep, then at least I can dream.   Marilyn Monroe

Marilyn Monroe

It is in our idleness, in our dreams, that the submerged truth sometimes comes to the top.   Virginia Woolf

Lose your dreams and you might lose your mind. It is unfulfilled dreams that keep you alive.   Mick Jagger

The mind loves the unknown. It loves images whose meaning is unknown, since the meaning of the mind itself is unknown.   René Magritte

The past is a great place and I don't want to erase it or to regret it, but I don't want to be its prisoner either. It is unfulfilled dreams that keep you alive.

Mick Jagger

Mick Jagger

In bed my real love has always been the sleep that rescued me by allowing me to dream.   Luigi Pirandello

Luigi Pirandello

Sometimes a cigar is just a cigar.   Sigmund Freud

A woman is an occasional pleasure but a cigar is always a smoke.

Groucho Marx

The strength of women comes from the fact that psychology cannot explain us. Men can be analysed, women merely adored.   Oscar Wilde

The great question that has never been answered, and which I have not yet been able to answer, despite my thirty years of research into the feminine soul, is "What does a woman want?"   Sigmund Freud

What a strange thing is man!
And what a stranger is woman!
What a whirlwind is her head
And what a whirlpool full of depth
And danger is all the rest about her.   Lord Byron

Men are governed by lines of intellect – women: by curves of emotion.
                                                                James Joyce

James Joyce

The true man wants two things: danger and play. For that reason he wants woman,
as the most dangerous plaything.   Friedrich Nietzsche

The desire of the man is for the woman, but the desire of the woman is for the
desire of the man.   Madame de Staël

Anyone who says he can see through women is missing a lot.   Groucho Marx

Let us leave pretty women to man devoid of imagination.   Marcel Proust

While I visited Nigeria this summer, my cousin Anayo talked about how the people over there believe in curses, voodoo magic, and crack cures for diseases. That
was when I came up with the Law of Inverse Proportion: The number of acts of
superstition being reported in a given area is inversely proportional to the number
of educated people residing therein. I came back to the States and found to my
delight that the law still holds.   Uche Akotaobi

Minds that are ill at ease are agitated by both hope and fear.   Ovid

Fear and I were born twins.   Thomas Hobbes

It is no longer a question of staying healthy. It's a question of finding a sickness you like.

Jackie Mason

Why waste money on psychotherapy when you can listen to the B Minor Mass?

Michael Torke

Neurosis is the natural, logical development of an individual who is comparatively inactive, filled with a personal, egocentric striving for superiority, and is therefore retarded in the development of his social interest, as we find regularly among the more passive pampered styles of life.

Alfred Adler

Guilt is the mafia of the mind.

Bob Mandel

The longer the excuse, the less likely it's the truth.

Robert Half

It is better to offer no excuse than a bad one.

George Washington

Our greatest foes, and whom we must chiefly combat, are within.

Miguel de Cervantes Saavedra

Miguel de Cervantes Saavedra

Addiction is an increasing desire for an act which gives less and less satisfaction.

Aldous Huxley

The world is for the most part, a collective madhouse, and practically everyone, however 'normal' his facade, is faking sanity.

John Astin

There is no psychiatrist in the world like a puppy licking your face.

Ben Williams

If you cut a thing up, of course it will smell. Hence, nothing raises such an infernal stink at last, as human psychology.   David Herbert Lawrence

I don't do drugs. I am drugs.   Salvador Dalí

At the age of six I wanted to be a cook. At seven I wanted to be Napoleon. And my ambition has been growing steadily ever since.   Salvador Dalí

Oh, if I only knew the way back, the lovely way back to the time when I was a child.   Klaus Groth

Klaus Groth

Everybody has got to die, but I have always believed an exception would be made in my case.   William Saroyan

The ruler's wrath is death.   William Warham, Archbishop of Canterbury

William Warham, Archbishop of Canterbury

The more I study religion the more I am convinced that man never worshipped anything but himself.   Richard Burton

Richard Burton

Religion is the satisfaction, for some, of PEN – personal emotional need – and nothing more.   Sir Arnold Wolfendale

When one's thoughts are neither frivolous nor flippant, when one's thoughts are neither stiff-necked nor stupid, but rather, are harmonious – they habitually render physical calm and deep insight.   Hildegard of Bingen

Love is the only dirty trick played on us by evolution to achieve the continuation of the species.   Anonymous

Love is like the measles; we all have to go through it.   Jerome K. Jerome

Love is the power to see similarity in the dissimilar.   Theodor W. Adorno

Theodor W. Adorno

To love oneself is the beginning of a lifelong romance.   Oscar Wilde

First, to be able to love, then to learn that body and spirit are one.

Hugo von Hofmannsthal

Hugo von Hofmannsthal

Nobody contributes to the amusement of a party more than those who are not present.   Carl von Ossietzky

Labour-saving devices just make us try to cram more pointless activities into each day, rather than doing the important thing, which is to enjoy our life.

Tom Hodgkinson

References

Most quotations have been taken form the following web pages (to be prefixed by `http://`):

```
quotations.home.worldnet.att.net/science.html
quotes.wordpress.com/
naturalscience.com/dsqhome.html
www.lhup.edu/~dsimanek/sciquote.htm
www-groups.dcs.st-and.ac.uk/~history/Quotations/
      Gauss.html
www.quotegarden.com/
www.wisdomquotes.com/cat_philosophy.html
quotes.prolix.nu/Quotations/
www.quotegarden.com/science.html
www.gdargaud.net/Humor/QuotesScience.html
www.some-guy.com/quotes/adams.html
www.5points.com/library/5quotes.htm
laserstars.org/bio/Feynman.html
www.sunion.warwick.ac.uk/modernscifi/library/
      hhgbooks.html
www.indianchild.com/Quotes/science_quotes.htm
www.brainyquote.com/
quotes.prolix.nu/Philosophy/
www.giga-usa.com/gigaweb1/quotes2/
      qutoppsychologyx001.htm
www.nonstopenglish.com/reading/quotations/
      k_Psychology.asp
www.nonstopenglish.com/reading/quotations/
      k_Psychiatry.asp
en.thinkexist.com/quotes/with/keyword/psychiatry/
home.att.net/~quotations/index.html#link
creatingminds.org/quotes/rationality.htm
www.wisdomquotes.com/cat_truth.html
```

www.stephenjaygould.org/ctrl/quotes_bigbang.html
atheism.about.com/library/quotes/bl_q_SHawking.htm
www.basicjokes.com/dquotes.php?cid=134
www.xmission.com/~dcc/quotes.html
gridtech.blogspot.com/2005_04_01_gridtech_archive.html
www.cs.virginia.edu/~robins/quotes.html
www.aip.org/history/newsletter/fall2001/
    photos-fall2001.htm
www.electrobionics.org/quote_ref.html
xona.com/quotes/inspirational.html
www.onlinekunst.de/zitate/zitate_verstehen.html
quote.joetoe.com/author/t.html
www.quoteland.com/
www.nytimes.com/
www.quotationspage.com/quotes/
www.scienceart.nl/Frames/Mainframes/Mainfr Quotes.htm
strangewondrous.net/browse/author/l/lovelace+ada
www.gap-system.org/~history/Quotations2/1210.html
www.icelebz.com/quotes/konrad_zuse/
en.wikipedia.org/wiki/Main_Page
www.studysoccer.com/terms/
    quote_by_ada_byron_lovelace.php

Author Index*

*Pages marked with a box superscript (□)
refer to portraits. Most informations on the
short CVs were inspired by and taken from
http://en.wikipedia.org/.

Allen, Arnold, 55
*1937(?); American instructor, public speaker, and writer; specialist in the analysis and mathematical modelling of computer performance

Allen, Woody, 36, 36□, 49, 91, 115, 206, 221, 265, 285
*1935; born as Allen Stewart Konigsberg; American screenwriter, film director, actor, comedian, writer, musician, and playwright

Alstad, Ken, 68
Contemporary author and expert on Lean and Meaty One-Liners

Althusius, Johannes, 127, 127□
1563–1638; German jurisconsult and Calvinist political philosopher

American Psychiatric Association, 259

Annan, Kofi, 24, 24□
*1938; 7th General Secretary of the United Nations; Nobel Prize for peace in 2001

Anonymous, 7, 35, 48, 72, 80, 88, 101, 111, 112, 116, 125, 256, 288, 297, 304

Anscombe, Elizabeth, 148, 148□
1919–2001; Gertrude Elizabeth Margaret Anscombe; British philosopher and theologian; student of Ludwig Wittgenstein

Anscombe, Francis John, 94
1918–2001; British statistician

Anselm of Canterbury, 191, 191□
1033–1109; Italian Benedictine monk and philosopher

Aquinas, St. Thomas, 131, 212, 216, 226, 226□, 248, 249, 292
1225–1274; Italian priest of the Catholic Church in the Dominican Order; immensely influential philosopher and theologian

Archimedes, 15
287–212 BC; Archimedes of Syracuse; Greek mathematician, physicist, and engineer

Arendt, Hannah, 133, 206, 235, 236, 236□
1906–1975; Jewish German–American journalist and scholar

Aristotle, 111, 126, 157, 166, 182, 213, 233, 235, 235□, 245
384–322 BC; Greek philosopher; student of Plato and teacher of Alexander the Great

Armstrong, Louis, 51, 51□
1901–1971; Louis Daniel 'Satchmo' Armstrong; American jazz musician (trumpet player) and vocalist

Arp, Hans, 260, 260□
1886–1966; German–French painter, sculptor, and lyric poet

Artaud, Antonin, 282
1896–1948; French poet, essayist, playwright, and actor

Asimov, Isaac, 12, 37, 41, 104, 242
1920–1992; Russian–American biochemist and very productive science-fiction author

Assisi, St. Francis of, 220, 222, 222□
1182–1226; Giovanni Francesco di Bernardone; Catholic deacon and preacher; founder of the Order of Friars Minor, more commonly known as the Franciscans

Astaire, Fred, 124
1899–1987; originally Frederick Austerlitz; US-American dancer and actor

Astin, John, 302
*1930; US-American actor and stage director

Attenborough, Lord Samuel Richard, 179
*1923; British actor and stage director

Auden, Wystan Hugh, 283
1907–1973; British and since 1946 American writer

Augustus, 125, 125□
63 BC–14 AC; first Roman emperor

Avicenna, 93, 115, 115□
980–1037; Arab.: Ibn Sina; Persian physician, physicist, philosopher, lawyer, mathematician, and alchemist

Babbage, Charles, 59, 59□, 80, 131
1791–1871; British reformer, mathematician, computer pioneer, economist, mechanical engineer, code-breaker, and inventor

Bacon, Francis, 63, 96, 96□, 113, 121, 157, 158, 177, 177□, 289, 289□, 290
1561–1626; British philosopher and politician

Bacon, Roger, 85, 182
1214–1292 or 1294; called Doctor Mirabilis; British monk of the Franciscans and philosopher

Baez, Joan, 138, 285
*1941; US-American folk singer with strong political engagement

Bagehot, Walter, 28, 44
1826–1877; British economist, expert on constitutions, and editor of the weekly journal "The Economist"

Bahn, Pat, 183
American aerospace consultant

Quotation Beginnings

All the choir of Heaven and furniture of Earth ..., 189
All the effects of nature ..., 50
All the harmonies of creation ..., 28
All the physics you have learned ..., 82
All the reasonings of men ..., 269
All the resources we need ..., 154
All theoretical chemistry is really physics ..., 115
All truth passes through three stages. ..., 181
All truths are easy to understand ..., 41
Almost everyone who didn't know what to do ..., 157
Alone the fact that we exist ..., 135
Although a skillful flatterer is a most delightful companion ..., 254
Although God demands a whole heart ..., 132
Although most people never overcome ..., 153
Always be a first-rate version of yourself ..., 271
Always laugh when you can. ..., 278
Always tell the truth. ..., 246
Amazing Electronic Fact: ..., 115
An actual stroll through a lunatic asylum ..., 276
An alcoholic is ..., 288
An anagram for astronomer: ..., 111
An army of deer lead by a lion ..., 176
An atheist is someone ..., 147
An audience is never wrong. ..., 264
An essential aspect of creativity ..., 152
An experiment at the All-India Institute of Mental Health ..., 259
An experiment is a question ..., 11
An extremely healthy dose of skepticism ..., 64
An eye for an eye ..., 126
An object in possession ..., 212
An ounce of action ..., 243
Ancient metaphysics underwent many changes ..., 230
And indeed we believe you ..., 191
And soon, too soon, we part with pain ..., 219
And those whose hearts are fixed on reality ..., 228
And thought struggles against the results ..., 85
Animals have these advantages over man ..., 52

Anticipate charity ..., 200
Any crooked bookkeeper's books ..., 223
Any man who reads too much ..., 213
Any philosophy that can be put in a nutshell ..., 186
Any small object that is accidentally dropped ..., 113
Any sufficiently advanced technology ..., 83
Any two philosophers can tell each other ..., 186
Anybody can do bad work ..., 236
Anybody who is 25 or 30 years old ..., 184
Anyone can hold the helm ..., 66
Anyone who attempts to generate random numbers ..., 105
Anyone who believes in science ..., 72
Anyone who cannot come to terms ..., 261
Anyone who cannot cope with mathematics ..., 47
Anyone who expects a source of power from ..., 100
Anyone who goes to a psychiatrist ..., 272
Anyone who has never made a mistake ..., 83
Anyone who hates dogs and kids ..., 265
Anyone who says ..., 301
Anyone who seeks to destroy the passions ..., 286
Anyone who stops learning is old ..., 182
Anything becomes interesting ..., 84
Anything that is too stupid ..., 217
Apart from the known and the unknown ..., 157
Are quarks and gluons the Platonic ideas of ..., 198
Are the four dimensions ..., 110
Arriving at one goal ..., 173
Art does not reproduce the visible; ..., 209
Art is a jealous mistress ..., 258
Art is a marriage ..., 151
Art is the daughter ..., 203
As a cure for worrying ..., 196
As a matter of fact, mathematics is a science ..., 81
As contraries are known by contraries ..., 293
As far as the laws of mathematics refer to reality ..., 50
As long as a word remains unspoken ..., 165
As long as algebra and geometry ..., 17
As physics advances farther and farther ..., 96

Every form of addiction is bad ... , 263
Every government is run by liars ... , 155
Every law is an infraction ... , 128
Every man takes the limits ... , 234
Every science begins as philosophy ... , 203
Every time you smile at someone ... , 274
Every true man ... , 162
Every wave, regardless of how high ... , 209
Everybody gets so much information ... , 169
Everybody has got to die ... , 303
Everyone has his dark side ... , 34
Everyone is a moon ... , 221
Everyone wants to have a friend ... , 273
Everything great in the world ... , 241
Everything has been figured out ... , 220
Everything has been said ... , 211
Everything is relative. ... , 189
Everything that irritates us ... , 263
Everything that is really great ... , 198
Everything that occurs ... , 28
Everything that you could possibly imagine
    ... , 64
Everything you imagine is real., 113
Everything you've learned in school ... , 35
Everywhere, we learn only from those ... , 216
Evil deeds do not prosper; ... , 237
Evolution, of course, is not something ... , 24
Evolutionary cosmology formulates ... , 18
Example is not the main thing ... , 179
Examples ... which might be multiplied ad
    libitum ... , 110
Experience by itself is not science., 89
Experience has shown ... , 227
Experience is directly proportional to ... , 245
Exposing students to the history of science ... ,
    59
Extraordinary claims demand extraordinary
    proof. ... , 265

Facts are many ... , 245
Facts can be turned into art ... , 203
Facts do not cease to exist ... , 186
Facts speak louder ... , 93
Facts themselves are meaningless. ... , 109
Failure is instructive. ... , 173
Failure is only the opportunity ... , 173
Falsehood is easy ... , 246
Famous last words: ... , 18

Famous remarks are very seldom quoted
    correctly., 3
Fancy wordings ... , 3
Far too many people do not understand ... ,
    203
Fear and I were ... , 301
Feminine meekness ... , 268
Fermi devoted a great deal of his time to the
    graduate students ... , 55
Few are those who can see with their own eyes
    ... , 109
First learn the meaning of what you say ... ,
    203
First, to be able to love ... , 305
Follow where reason leads., 248
For a man to attain to an eminent degree ... ,
    173
For a successful technology ... , 60
For every complex problem ... , 98
For every one billion particles ... , 16
For example, justice is considered to mean
    equality. ... , 166
For fast acting relief ... , 67
For me the greatest beauty ... , 80
For my part, I wish all guns ... , 138
For Pleasure, Delight, Peace ... , 250
For the sake of making a living ... , 220
For the universe is infinite ... , 34
For to be free ... , 159
For truth is always strange; ... , 88
For us democracy is ... , 160
For who among men is he ... , 191
Formerly, when religion was strong ... , 282
Four things do not come back ... , 117
Fourth Law of Thermodynamics: ... , 102
Freedom is always and exclusively ... , 159
Freedom of conscience ... , 240
Freedom of thought ... , 156
Freud is the father ... , 284
Freudianism is much more nearly a religion
    ... , 258
Friendship is like an earthenware ... , 253
From a consideration of the immense volume
    ... , 15
From a moral point of view ... , 240
From henceforth, space by itself ... , 16
From now on there will be no physical treatise
    ... , 96
From reading too much ... , 173

Mathematics provides an invisible framework ..., 53

Mathematics, rightly viewed, possesses not only truth ..., 32

Mathematics: The alphabet God used ..., 31

[Max Planck] was one of the finest people I have ever known ..., 15

Maybe this world ..., 129

[Medicine is] a collection of uncertain prescriptions ..., 252

Medicine is not only a science; ..., 141

Medicine rests upon four pillars ..., 142

Mediocrity knows nothing ..., 175

Men and nations behave wisely ..., 174

Men are governed ..., 301

Men are like wine ..., 240

Men gladly believe ..., 288

Men ought to know ..., 163

Men who wish to know about the world ..., 63

Men will always be mad ..., 262

Mendicant orders and monks ..., 219

Mental health problems ..., 184

Metaphysics is a dark ocean ..., 231

Military intelligence is ..., 138

Military justice is ..., 138

Mind and matter in our little speck of the universe ..., 36

Minds that are ill at ease ..., 301

Miracles in the sense of events ..., 292

Misquotation is ..., 3

Modern psychology takes completely for granted ..., 65

Monarchy is the gold filling ..., 198

Money brings some happiness ..., 119

More than any other time in history ..., 49

Most institutions demand unqualified faith; ..., 126

Most of the evils of life ..., 239

Most of the vices and mortal sins ..., 259

Most people believe that sin ..., 259

Most people do not really want freedom ..., 66

Most truths are so naked ..., 88

Music in the soul ..., 217

Music is a higher revelation ..., 147

Music is always noise-related ..., 217

Music is the mediator ..., 272

Music was our wife ..., 290

My advice to you ..., 205

My brain is the key ..., 163

My friend, let's not think of tomorrow ..., 291

My present work concerns the problems ..., 23

My religion consists of a humble admiration ..., 195

My sources are unreliable ..., 3

My teacher, Hopkins, often commented ..., 150

My unconscious knows more ..., 297

My work has always tried to unite ..., 150

My writing is an answer ..., 131

Nations have their ego ..., 184

Natural objects, for example, must be experienced ..., 89

Natural science does not simply describe ..., 47

Natural science is ..., 243

Nature composes some of her loveliest poems ..., 7

Nature doesn't exist. ..., 102

Nature likes to hide itself., 103

Nature uses as little as possible ..., 92

Nature's laws govern which things can be done ..., 86

Neurosis is always a substitute ..., 275

Neurosis is no worse than a bad cold; ..., 263

Neurosis is the natural ..., 302

Neutrino physics is largely an art ..., 72

Neutrinos, they are very small ..., 73

Never believe anything in politics ..., 162

Never fear mighty men., 286

Never forget ..., 277

Never stand begging ..., 131

Newton's cosmology ..., 15

Night, the beloved. ..., 193

Ninety percent of the politicians ..., 292

No amount of experimentation can ever prove me right; ..., 87

No amount of skillful invention can replace ..., 62

No biodiversity without radioactivity., 91

No excellent soul is exempt ..., 233

No great improvements in the lot of mankind ..., 171

No human being can really understand another ..., 257

No human being is constituted to know the truth ..., 5

No human being will ever know the truth ..., 209

No known roof is as beautiful ..., 40

No language which lends itself to visualisability ..., 30

No man ever steps in the same river twice ..., 125

No man has a good enough memory ..., 64

No matter how wonderful our new technology is ..., 83

No miracle has ever taken place ..., 292

No nation has ever prospered ..., 138

No observations are absolutely trustworthy., 94

No one can be a great thinker ..., 172

No peace among the nations ..., 161

No people do so much harm ..., 224

No point is more central than this ..., 18

No progress without mutation., 91

No psychologist should pretend ..., 283

No snowflake in the avalanche ..., 223

Noble deeds and hot baths ..., 265

Nobody contributes to the amusement ..., 305

Nobody knows why ..., 86

Nobody, as long as he moves about ..., 67

Non-violence is a flop. ..., 138

Normal love isn't interesting. ..., 294

Not a shred of evidence exists ..., 261

Not everything that can be counted counts ..., 109

Nothing can be more real ..., 236

Nothing exists except atoms and empty space ..., 86

Nothing happens to you ..., 66

Nothing is easier than self-deceit. ..., 289

Nothing is easier than to break a taboo ..., 274

Nothing is ever accomplished ..., 239

Nothing is funnier than unhappiness ..., 275

Nothing is more astounding than the truth ..., 186

Nothing is more difficult ..., 63

Nothing is more responsible ..., 66

Nothing is often a good thing to do ..., 176

Nothing is politically right ..., 155

Nothing is so good ..., 250

Nothing is so wonderful ..., 273

Nothing is too wonderful to be true ..., 90

Nothing makes one feel so strong ..., 274

Nothing new can be created in the Universe ..., 33

Nothing tends so much to the advancement of knowledge ..., 60

Nothing travels faster than the speed of light ..., 115

Now I believe I can hear the philosophers ..., 142

Now it is established in the sciences ..., 93

Now it is quite clear to me ..., 6

Now there is one outstandingly important fact ..., 51

Now, my own suspicion is that the universe ..., 14

Nowadays the rage for possession ..., 119

Nuclear physics is interesting ..., 91

O how small a portion of earth ..., 176

Observations always involve theory. ..., 72

Obstacles are those frightful things ..., 169

Obstacles are what you see ..., 60

Odd how the creative power ..., 14

Of all political ideas ..., 175

Of course one should not drink much ..., 288

Of course, Einstein was a very great scientist indeed ..., 56

Of course, nobody would deny the importance of human beings ..., 29

Of the 'real' universe we know nothing ..., 34

Of the general theory of relativity ..., 29

Office jobs are physically easier ..., 253

Oh, if I only knew the way back ..., 303

OK, so what's the speed of dark?, 83

OK, so you're a Ph.D. ..., 101

On black holes: ..., 89

On the naming of the neutrino ..., 72

Once during a mass ..., 41

Once the realisation is accepted ..., 234

One cannot escape the feeling ..., 33

One does not have to appeal to God ..., 21

One foot is short; ..., 92

One machine can do the work of fifty ordinary men. ..., 260

One man's noise is another man's signal., 6

One may understand the cosmos ..., 34

One never notices what has been done; ..., 134

One never really knows ..., 241

One of Crete's own prophets has said it: ..., 235

One of my favorite philosophical tenets ..., 232

There comes a time when the mind takes a
    higher plane of knowledge . . . , 102
There is a simple grandeur in the view of life
    . . . , 135
There is a theory which states . . . , 32
There is a very narrow line . . . , 213
There is a wisdom of the head . . . , 227
There is absolutely no criterion for truth. . . . ,
    221
There is geometry in the humming of the
    strings . . . , 17
There is inherent in nature a hidden harmony
    . . . , 94
There is little difference between man . . . , 166
There is more information . . . , 37
There is more to life . . . , 60
There is no adequate defense . . . , 78
There is no doubt that human survival will
    continue . . . , 53
There is no evil in the atom; . . . , 191
There is no fun in doing nothing . . . , 295
There is no great genius . . . , 212
There is no law governing all things., 24
There is no likelihood . . . , 70
There is no national science . . . , 75
There is no psychiatrist . . . , 302
There is no psychology; . . . , 281
There is no record in human history . . . , 212
There is no statement so absurd . . . , 180
There is no worse screen . . . , 204
There is not one blade of grass . . . , 199
There is not past, no future; . . . , 184
There is nothing more wonderful . . . , 270
There is nothing new to be discovered . . . , 96
There is nothing permanent . . . , 156
There is nothing to it being an honest man . . . ,
    137
There is only one thing a philosopher can be
    . . . , 212
There is point in speaking of knowledge . . . ,
    148
There will be no end to the troubles . . . , 203
There will be no veterans . . . , 137
There's enough uncertainty about marriage . . . ,
    253
There's no sense in being precise . . . , 108
There's no system foolproof enough . . . , 86
There's nothing that can help you understand
    . . . , 244

Thermodynamics is a funny subject. . . . , 102
They say that something as small as a butterfly
    . . . , 93
They teach anything in universities . . . , 124
Think slow, act fast., 74
Thinking begins only . . . , 248
Thinking, we shape the objects . . . , 288
This century has been so rich in discovery . . . ,
    97
This is my simple religion. . . . , 161
This is the precept by which I have lived: . . . ,
    235
This is the way the world ends . . . , 223
This isn't right. . . . , 97
This question is too good . . . , 232
This universe is not hostile . . . , 22
This world, after all our science and sciences,
    . . . , 82
Those who are not shocked by quantum theory
    . . . , 108
Those who do not move . . . , 129
Those who educate children . . . , 235
Those who love something . . . , 206
Thou hast seen nothing yet. . . . , 145
Though we travel the world over . . . , 274
Thousands have gone to heaven . . . , 219
Thousands of candles can be lit . . . , 209
Three things cannot be long hidden: . . . , 106
Three-quarters of the sicknesses of intelligent
    people . . . , 259
Thus, the task is, not so much to see . . . , 69
Time is a fourth dimension . . . , 27
Time is nature's way of making certain . . . , 91
Time spent with cats . . . , 281
To argue with a person . . . , 141
To be a critic is a stupid job . . . , 148
To be a philosopher is . . . , 158
To be a philosophical skeptic . . . , 219
To be caught between two stools . . . , 137
To be conscious that you are ignorant . . . , 111
To be good is noble . . . , 164
To be ignorant of one's ignorance . . . , 165
To be is to be perceived., 189
To be successful, a woman has . . . , 268
To be too conscious is an illness . . . , 265
To climb steep hills . . . , 66
To comply heroic . . . , 162
To enjoy freedom . . . , 178
To enjoy the world . . . , 136

Subject Index